WE HAVE REASON TO BELIEVE

WE HAVE REASON TO BELIEVE

some aspects of Jewish theology examined
in the light of modern thought

RABBI LOUIS JACOBS

Fifth expanded edition

VALLENTINE MITCHELL
LONDON • PORTLAND, OR

This expanded edition
first published in 2004 in Great Britain by
VALLENTINE MITCHELL
Suite 314, Premier House
Edgware, Middlesex HA8 7BJ

and in the United States of America by
VALLENTINE MITCHELL
c/o ISBS, 920 NE 58th Avenue, Suite 300
Portland, Oregon 97213-3786

Website: www.vmbooks.com

British Library Cataloguing in Publication Data
has been applied for

Library of Congress Cataloging in Publication Data
has been applied for

ISBN: 0 85303 538 5 (cloth)
ISBN: 978 0 85303 538 1
ISBN: 0 85303 560 1 (paper)
ISBN: 978 0 85303 560 2

Printed in Great Britain by Biddles Ltd, King's Lynn, Norfolk

For Shulamith,
my wife

Acknowledgements

A SMALL part of the material published here has appeared in article form in the *Jewish Chronicle, Menorah, The Jewish Spectator* and the *A.J.A. Quarterly*, whose editors I wish to thank.

I am deeply indebted to a number of friends: to William Frankel for his ready help and unfailing encouragement, to Ian Gordon for suggesting the title and for many hours of fruitful discussion, to Lawrence Jacobs and Alan Jacobs for their keen interest in the production of this book, to Michael Edwardes for reading the manuscript and for his valuable suggestions; and to the members of my congregation and Study Group, whose interest in Judaism has been a constant stimulus.

L.J.

Contents

A Retrospect of the 'Jacobs Affair'

This book, based on discussions of a study group conducted at the New West End Synagogue, where I functioned as the Minister-Preacher (a quaint title preferred for 'Rabbi' by the United Synagogue in 1954 at the time of my appointment), was first published in 1957 by Vallentine Mitchell, of which publishing house Frank Cass was (and happily still is) the director. The book received little attention until the 'Jacobs Affair' of which it was the catalyst. A second edition was published in 1962, when the early rumblings of the 'Affair' were beginning to be heard. Once the 'Affair' had fully erupted, a third edition was published, in 1965, to which an Epilogue was appended in which I essayed to provide an elaboration and defence of my views. To the fourth edition, published in 1995, a Preface was added containing further elaborations. To the present reprint of this edition Frank Cass has urged me to supply this Retrospect and, although by now I am becoming thoroughly fed up with having to explain and defend my views again and again, for Frank Cass, who has been a source of great encouragement for so many years, to command is for me to obey. This is not, I hope, a mere rehash but a retrospect in which I try, unsuccessfully no doubt, to avoid the element of self-indulgence critics have detected in the oft-repeated surveys, forced upon me, when returning to my thoughts in the past.

Here is the place to mention that this Retrospect also takes into account my autobiography, *Helping With Inquiries*, also published by Vallentine Mitchell, 1989; *God Torah Israel – Traditionalism Without Fundamentalism*, Hebrew Union College Press, Cincinnati, 1990; and *Beyond Reasonable Doubt*, Littman Library, 1990. I described the last work as a sequel to *We Have Reason to Believe*. I have also treated the theme of understanding revelation in the light of modern thought in other of my works on Jewish theology.

The thesis of the book, for which it was attacked from the right and left, each from its own point of view, is that modern knowledge and scholarship have made it impossible to accept the traditional view that God 'dictated' to Moses, word for word and letter by letter, the whole of the Pentateuch (the Torah). My argument runs that, while such a doctrine of verbal inspiration is now untenable, the traditional doctrine that the Torah is from Heaven can and should still be maintained. To put this in different words, God *is* the author of the Torah (conceived of as the sum total not of the Pentateuch alone but of Jewish religious thought through the ages), but, as in His creativity in the world, He cooperated with His creatures in producing the Torah, through human beings reaching out to Him. There is thus a human element, as well as a divine element, in what we call the Torah.

That the notion of direct divine communication, for all its hallowed history, has had to be abandoned is demanded by our present-day knowledge. The findings of geology, astronomy, archaeology, biblical criticism and modern research into the sources of Judaism all go to show that Judaism ('the Torah') has undergone development as Jews came into contact with and were influenced by societies and cultures different from their own.

Reform and Liberal theologians have been largely puzzled that all this is in any way a source of offence. 'So what else is new?' they exclaim. Human beings have known for centuries that, as Galileo said after his recantation, 'The earth still moves.' My reply has been that I have never tried to present as new the findings of science and the modern historical approach. Nothing could be more absurd. I have only tried to put forward the view, a big 'only' to be sure, that Jewish practice, the Halakhah, is still binding because this is the will of God, provided, of course, that the Torah is seen, as it often is in the tradition itself, in dynamic terms of trial and error, falsehood gradually yielding to truth, with God involved in the whole process. Nor do I claim any originality for such a view, which has been held by Jewish religious traditionalists from the early nineteenth century, and which lies behind the attitude, I would maintain, of many religious Jews today. But I now admit that I was wrong in imagining that such views are compatible with Orthodoxy as this is now understood in fundamentalist terms. (I use 'fundamentalism' not in a pejorative sense but only to denote the attitude of those who are either indifferent or antagonistic to all modern critical scholarship.) Yet some Liberal thinkers – particularly, in this country, Rabbi John Rayner, whose honesty and integrity I respect – have faulted me for not going far enough in advocating more radical changes in the Halakhah. I have tried to deal with this subject in my book *A Tree of Life*, referred to in the Preface to this edition.

So far as Orthodox reaction to the book is concerned, the Charedi world and the Yeshivah world pursue their own way and never discuss in writing the kind of theological and historical questions I consider, and a book such as mine leaves them cold. As for the Modern Orthodox, these thinkers somehow manage to combine total acceptance of the critical historical approach with regard to the other parts in the Bible with a completely fundamentalistic acceptance of divine 'dictation of the Pentateuch' to Moses. I want to give a number of examples of how outstanding Modern Orthodox scholars and thinkers go to extraordinary lengths in their attempt to reconcile the doctrine of divine dictation to Moses in ways that are themselves amazingly untraditional and can satisfy neither traditionalists nor modernists.

In a review of my book *Beyond Reasonable Double*, Dr Tamar Roth of Bar-Ilan University asks why I ignore the ideas put forward by David Weiss Halivni and Mordecai Breuer. Her review appeared in *Studies in Contemporary Jewry* (Israel), Vol. 18, 2002. I had met Dr Roth at *Limmud* and had an interesting conversation with her on Orthodoxy and criticism during which I asked her why no Modern Orthodox scholars ever come out with the kind of views on the challenge from Biblical criticism I have been dealing with over these many years. She replied that some of them do, and that I should wait and see. In this review she refers me to Halivni (*Revelation Restored: Divine Writ and Critical Responses*, Westview Press, Boulder, CO, 1997) and to Mordecai Breuer ('Torah Min Ha-Shammayin', offprint from *Megadim*, 32, Shevat 761–2001). Dr Roth remarks further that I have too readily waved aside Rav Kook, who accepts the theory of evolution as compatible with Genesis. I had failed to see how Kook's theory is compatible with the story of Adam and Eve. In fact, Dr Roth says, Rav Kook came very close to declaring the Adam story a myth. Kook may have come very close to this but where, in all his writings, does he do so? The use of the word 'myth' is never faced by Rav Kook and could not have been, since he and many other Modern Orthodox scholars who follow him have no use for theories derived from modern biblical scholarship.

David Weiss Halivni is a famed scholar and teacher, applying with great skill the critical historical method, of which he is an undisputed master, to the talmudic literature, especially to textual and form criticism. In his personal life Professor Weiss is strictly Orthodox. Not surprising, therefore, is his attempt to reconcile biblical criticism with the doctrine of Torah Min Ha-Shammayim, which he identifies with the belief that God gave the Torah to Moses. His thesis involves the idea that the original Torah imparted by God to Moses became obscured during the course of transmission through the later generations. The original text was commented on and constantly transformed so that the final text of the Torah as we now have it is the work of Ezra, who edited the whole corpus that had come down to him. The critics who detect contradictions and inconsistencies in the Pentateuch are right from one point of view, but these are the result of the constant reworking of the original text. Halivni is evidently unable to suggest, as I do, that the doctrine of Torah Min Ha-Shammayim means that the critical discoveries of diverse stands in the Pentateuch demand that the Torah is seen as the outcome of the various sources and the editorial processes of combing them. No, says Halivni, if I understand him correctly for that would involve too radical a departure from the traditional view that God conveyed the Torah directly to Moses. But, if the traditional view is to be invoked, it is that the *whole* of the Torah was given by God to Moses, not just a part of it. Halivni not only fails to detect the supposed original text of the Torah but, in the process, he is just as untraditional as I am. What is called for is a reinterpretation of the tradition in the light of the 'assured results' of critical researches which Halivni himself seems to regard as assured. Halivni's view has not won much acceptance among the Modern Orthodox.

Breuer's attempt at reconciliation is more puzzling than

Halivni's. At the beginning of the 'Jacob Affair' many years ago, a writer in the *Jewish Chronicle* compared Breuer's view – that the critics were right in detecting diverse sources in the Torah – with mine, and the writer remarked that a Rosh Yeshivah in Israel, as Breuer was at that time, could get away with it without theological obloquy while a London rabbi (me) was banned from Orthodoxy. Breuer wrote to the paper protesting that his view was entirely different from mine. In his much more recent article Breuer remarks that he has had the opportunity to study my views in much greater detail, and now feels that my description of the critical view is accurate so far as it goes. What, then, is one to make of the doctrine that God 'wrote' (presumably Breuer means 'conveyed' or 'dictated') the Torah to Moses? Breuer's incredible reply is that God, the author of all creation, knew that the various strands with their contradictions would eventually appear, and that these foreseen elements and categories were all conveyed by God to Moses. Thus, if the documentary hypothesis is correct, J.D.E. and P. actually exist but all four were given by God to Moses. There is no problem with God, the ruler of all, facing contradictions since in our experience of God's providential care there are the 'contradictions' between justice and mercy.

Breuer's method of dealing with anachronisms in the Torah is weird. In the Middle Ages, Abraham Ibn Ezra detected post-Mosaic additions to the Pentateuch, one of which is the verse 'and pursued as far as Dan' (Genesis 14:14). There was no city with the name of Dan in the time of Moses since the city's name is based on the territory of the tribe of Dan, which means that it was called Dan only after this tribe had settled in the land. Breuer, true to his theory, argues that God could have recorded the name of a city that would be given only after Moses and that He 'dictated' this name to Moses even though at the time of Moses the name would have been unintelligible.

The main point I wish to make is that defenders of the 'traditional' view such as Halivni and Breuer are themselves highly untraditional. Nowhere before Halivni did any Jewish sage postulate that only an unidentifiable part of the Torah was given by God to Moses (Halivni), or that the Torah was given in diverse strands only to be recovered later in history (Breuer).

Perhaps the most startling departure from tradition in the name of tradition is provided by Shubert Spero, a leading Modern Orthodox rabbi, teacher and theologian, also, now, of Bar-Ilan University. Spero's article 'The Biblical Stories of Creation, Garden of Eden and the Flood: History or Metaphor?' appeared in the Orthodox journal *Tradition*, 32, 2, 1999. Although it was criticised by writers in the next issue of the journal, together with Spero's replies to his critics, the editor saw no objection to Spero's thesis on the grounds of unorthodox belief. Spero is certainly not so naive as to identify the six days of the creation narrative with long periods of time, but treats the whole creation narrative as a metaphorical account of how the world and man within it emerged. He speaks of the 'big bang' theory and of Neanderthals and the many strains of pre-humans before *Homo sapiens* emerged. Spero goes on in this striking article calmly to postulate that the stories of Adam and Eve and the flood are best understood as 'metaphor' or *mashal* (he never uses the word 'myth').

Spero contends that the story of Adam and Eve is not an account of what actually happened but is precisely that: a story. We are obliged, as Orthodox Jews, Spero says, to take the commandments of the Torah as real commands, but the stories of Adam and Eve and the strange fruit of the garden, the tragic heroine and the speaking snake, bear all the marks of a parable pointing to features of God's creative activity. The sam applies to the otherwise unrealistic story of Noah's Art and the flood, in which all mankind is destroyed and only a single family is saved in a box it took over a hundred years to build and into which all the animals entered two by two to be saved in order to replenish the earth. In Spero's view the central features contained in the narrative are hints of the creative processes from the 'big bang' to the great successive upheavals in nature which led to the preparation of the earth to become a suitable habitat for human beings with free choice and moral worth. When challenged by his critics that our rabbis speak of Noah and the generation of the flood as real persons, Spero can only reply that real persons can still be used as vehicles for a metaphorical account – just as, according to some Midrashic sources, in the Biblical story of Job the hero is both a real person and, at the same time, a *mashal*.

Here we have a noted Modern Orthodox thinker prepared to acknowledge that significant passages in the Torah are to be understood in a metaphorical sense. Now, in any present-day critical view, these stories are human stories by humans – inspired, if you will – who only had the science of their day, who operated with ancient accounts, paralleled in Babylonian myths which, nevertheless, culminated in Genesis in the life-giving, moral Torah. Spero cannot say this, since he operates with the idea that Torah Min Ha-Shammayim means that the whole of the Torah is God-given in a direct sense.

The Modern Orthodox theologians we have considered – Halivni, Breuer and Spero – all advance completely untraditional views on the meaning of divine revelation, so that they might as well have advocated the admittedly untraditional view that divine revelation takes place through inspired human beings who, over a long period of time, cooperated with God in producing the glory that is called the Torah. This has been my complaint. Modern Orthodoxy has not rejected the critical, historical methodology with regard to such questions as the authorship and meaning of other parts of scripture. They accept that King David did not write the Psalm, that King Solomon is not the author of Ecclesiastes, that there is a Deutero-Isaiah and that the doctrine of the oral Torah embraces the rabbinic developments of the Torah, produced by great sages to be sure, but human beings nonetheless. And yet they continue to refuse to maintain that the Pentateuch can be understood in anything save in a fundamentalist sense of divine dictation to Moses. It is not only that modernists are not allowed to disagree with Maimonides' formulation in a pre-critical and pre-modern age, but that Maimonides' formulation does not allow for the view that we have only an unidentified part of the origin of Torah, that the Torah was given in differences of style, language and background or that some of the most important passages are to be understood as metaphor. In other words, where is the logic in departing from Maimonides in understanding the nature of the Torah and yet accepting the view of the greatest of our teacher's formulation that it is no longer true to modern thought?

So much for theory. On a practical level my views may have been considered to be heretical, but I know from personal contact through the years that many of the Modern Orthodox and even a few of the Charedim have shown sufficient interest in my view to whisper in my ear: 'There is something in what you are saying.'

In Anglo-Jewry, however, the Orthodox establishment and the Chief Rabbi have have dubbed me a heretic. The Chief Rabbi has never responded to my critique of Modern Orthodoxy. On Torah Min Ha-Shammayim, he has never stated explicitly where his view diverges from mine. He often seems to imply that he accepts some kind of development theory, as when he says repeatedly that it is essential for Orthodox Jews to believe that in the Mosaic Books (sic) we have the unmediated word of God. Why not in the Torah or in the Chumash? The expression 'Mosaic Books' lends itself to the notion of developmental theory – that is, as meaning that the five books came to be *attributed* to Moses. More than once I have urged the Chief Rabbi to declare that basically his views differ only slightly from mine, but he has not bothered to reply.

And there is the odd matter of the London Beth Din issuing a ruling to the effect that while I am welcome to any United Synagogue as a congregant, I cannot be called up to the Torah because, granted my beliefs, I cannot honestly recite the benediction: 'Who has chosen us from all peoples and given us His Torah.' But I am allowed, I was told, to open the Ark. An Orthodox journal thus explained the inconsistency that opening the Ark is a 'non-speaking part', as if the synagogue service were a film in which I could be an extra but never have a starring role.

If, as a result of the above, I find myself, over forty years after the publication of *We Have Reason to Believe*, in something of an Anglo-Jewish limbo, belonging neither to the Orthodox nor to the Reform, nor, in a sense, fully to the Masorti, I do not complain. I suppose I asked for it. I have consoled myself by quoting a Hasidic saying which runs: 'One who has no place anywhere has a place everywhere.' I have had and still have friends in all camps. Also to be recognised is the fact that the milder attitudes which still prevailed in Anglo-Jewry forty years ago have hardened and become more rigid so far as the Orthodox are concerned. If Jews' College still existed – alas, it does not – I would not have been accepted as a lecturer, let alone as Principal of the Institution. Many of today's Orthodox rabbis are products of Yeshivah education or come from Lubavitch and can hardly be described as 'modern' and, with few notable exceptions, have little training in modern historical scholarship.

Looking back is often hazardous. See what happened to Lot's wife! But I think I can honestly say that I have not turned into a pillar of salt, have not felt much rancour and have certainly not become bitter. On the contrary, I now see that the whole thing, so far as I am concerned, has been an exciting, worthwhile adventure.

For going over old ground I must apologise by repeating a story I have often told in my lectures. An old Jew was observed in a railway carriage muttering to himself and waving his hands in dismissive gestures from time to time. 'What are you doing?' he was asked. 'I was bored with the long journey and was telling myself Jewish jokes to while away the time.' 'And why did you wave your hands?' 'I have heard them all before.'

Preface to the Fifth Edition
by William Frankel, CBE

The 'Jacobs Affairs' – in fact, there were two of them – in a way crystallised my own religious attitudes. I have always had an emotional attachment to traditional Judaism, stemming from the cosiness and warmth of my own religious background. But, as I moved out of this comfortable womb, beginning when I first attended a school which did not have a preponderance of Jewish pupils, I recognised that some of the beliefs and practices of the faith in which I had been nurtured appeared to conflict with what I was learning and what was generally accepted among educated people. The Pentateuch, I had been taught at home, in the synagogue and in cheder, was the actual word of God and therefore could not be challenged, but in school I had learned something about Darwin and evolution. Both could not be true.

However, there wasn't much I could do about it, nor was the problem so intense as to call for some action on my part. The old-fashioned rabbis with whom I was acquainted through the synagogues which I attended with my father did not know enough about secular studies to understand the questions, let alone possess the ability to answer them. The more modern Orthodox rabbis tended to take the line that beliefs were less important than the practice of a Jewish way of life and the performance of the *mitzvot*. At that time, my only acquaintance with what is now called Progressive Judaism was the Liberal service conducted by Basil Henriques on Friday evenings at Berner Street School, where he ran the Bernhard Baron Jewish Settlement after school hours. I attended once, and found the predominantly English service rather bizarre, more akin to the church rituals I had sometimes seen in the cinema than to the all-Hebrew prayers of the Orthodox synagogues with which I was familiar.

My traditional loyalties remained paramount and, although my intelligence wasn't really satisfied by the observances I performed, I was too busy doing things to be overly concerned with my growing perplexity. Beliefs and unsophisticated Bible criticism were not subjects for discussion in my youthful environment. I suppose I became what David Daube, whom I met some years later in Cambridge, described as 'Orthoprax' rather than Orthodox. But I could not escape the issue or tradition-versus-reason when I became involved with Rabbi Jacobs.

Louis Jacobs, the only son of working-class parents in Manchester, showed an early aptitude for rabbinic studies. He was the bright boy of the Manchester yeshivah at which he became a full-time student and, at the instigation of his teachers, Louis's parents allowed him to undertake advanced rabbinical studies at the kollel, the scholarly rabbinic centre of East European-type Orthodoxy, in Gateshead. At the same time, or soon after, he pursued secular studies at the University of London and gained both bachelor and doctoral degrees.

He became the darling of Anglo-Jewish Orthodoxy and greatness was predicted for him. His rabbinic scholarship, wide reading, retentive memory and clarity of expression made him, while still in the very early years of his rabbinical career, talked about as a future Chief Rabbi.

When, in 1953, Rabbi Dr Louis Jacobs, then in his mid-thirties, accepted a 'call' to the pulpit of the New West End Synagogue in London, it came as a shock to the Orthodox community, for the Anglicised New West End was on the left wing of the United Synagogue. It had a tradition of mild reform, symbolised by its mixed choir – anathema to the strictly Orthodox. The membership of the New West End Synagogue included such luminaries as Viscount Samuel, Lord (Simon) Marks of Marks & Spencer fame, and the president of the United Synagogue, the Hon. Ewen Montagu, QC. Becoming the rabbi of such a synagogue made Jacobs suspect in the eyes of the Orthodox militants. I was a board member and former warden of the New West End when Jacobs arrived and, because of my activity in the synagogue, we saw a great deal of each other and became good friends. At the time of his appointment, I was still practising at the Bar.

Very early in his new pulpit, Louis delivered a series of sermons on Jewish prayer which impressed me greatly. By that time, I had become the general manager of the *Jewish*

Chronicle and I offered to publish them under the imprint of Jewish Chronicle Publications. He was happy about that and the booklet did rather well, particularly in the United States. It was his first publication and its success inspired him to more writings.

A while later he gave me the manuscript of a book entitled *We Have Reason to Believe*, which had emerged out of a discussion group he had led at the synagogue. It was intended as a modern kind of guide to the perplexed (though Jacobs himself never claimed it to be such) and his thesis was that true belief did not demand an abdication of reason. He took the position that, although faith is above reason, those elements of religion which were capable of being tested should not be exempt from scholarly inquiry. As a result, he concluded that Judaism had to accept the fact that the Bible was the work of human beings, albeit divinely inspired.

I read the manuscript and invited Louis to come over and talk about it. I told him that I thought it an important book and was sure that Vallentine Mitchell (the publishing subsidiary of the *Jewish Chronicle*) would publish it. But I advised against early publication. The reason was that the retirement of Dr Israel Brodie, then the Chief Rabbi, was expected in the next year or two. I had no doubt that Louis would be a strong candidate, but I took the view that early publication of the book would provide ammunition to the right-wingers likely to oppose his appointment. Why not wait until after the event and publish then?

Louis, however, was adamant. He did not want to wait and, if his views were likely to be controversial, he thought it right that they should be known before his name was considered rather than be disclosed afterwards. I naturally deferred to his opinion, and the book was duly published in 1957.

I still believe that, if publication had been delayed, Louis would, in all likelihood, have been appointed Chief Rabbi and the religious nature of the Anglo-Jewish community would have differed profoundly from what it became.

In fact, the book did not create an immediate stir and was well received by all sections of the community, including the Orthodox. The reviews were good: the organ of the Mizrachi, the religious Zionist party, enthused about it as the modern man's guide to Jewish Orthodoxy. (I was amused some years later, when the Jacobs Affair Part One had begun, that the same journal refused to accept an advertisement for *We Have Reason to Believe* consisting of extracts from its own review.)

I had been visiting the United States regularly since 1947 and had made the acquaintance of Louis Finkelstein, the chancellor of the Jewish Theological Seminary of America. The JTS was the intellectual and spiritual centre of American Conservative Judaism, a movement adhering to the Jewish tradition but recognising the necessity for change. Ironically, in the light of subsequent developments, the ethos of the JTS was created by its first chancellor, Dr Solomon Schechter, who came from England and brought with him the concept of 'progressive conservatism', then the slogan of the United Synagogue, which later rejected Louis Jacobs for propounding the same philosophy.

Louis Finkelstein visited London every summer to work at the British Museum, staying at an unpretentious hotel in that neighbourhood. Some time towards the end of the 1950s, I introduced him to Louis Jacobs, who greatly impressed the American scholar and, in 1959, the American Louis offered the British Louis a senior appointment on the academic staff of the JTS.

It was an extremely attractive offer, for the JTS faculty included some of the most illustrious names in Jewish scholarship, among them Louis Ginzburg, Saul Lieberman, Abraham Joshua Heschel and Louis Finkelstein himself. To join that company was an irresistible temptation and Jacobs was ready to accept.

That saddened me. There was no other rabbi in Britain possessing Louis Jacobs's levels of Jewish and secular scholarship, as well as the intellectual honesty which made an appeal to the thinking Jew. I thought it would be an irreparable loss to the Anglo-Jewish community if he left and I discussed the problem with Ewen Montagu, president of the United Synagogue, who was a Jacobs admirer and also saw him as the next Chief Rabbi. Ewen was in complete agreement that we should try to keep Jacobs here, and we both thought that the best way of achieving that and preparing him for the Chief Rabbinate would be an appointment at Jews' College, the seminary for the training of the Orthodox Anglo-Jewish ministry.

The principal of the college at that time, Rabbi Dr Isidore Epstein, would reach the age of retirement in a few years and Jacobs would be a natural successor. Ewen agreed to put the proposal to Sir Alan Mocatta, then the president of the college, and later informed me that he had done so and had met with an immediate and positive response. Mocatta had then spoken to Chief Rabbi Israel Brodie who, under the constitution of the College, possessed a power of veto over its appointments. Brodie agreed to the appointment of Jacobs as moral tutor, and I am not quite sure now whether the proposal to appoint him as principal on Dr Epstein's retirement was put to him by Ewen Montagu at that time. But I did mention that aspect to Dr Solomon Gaon, the Haham of the Spanish & Portuguese community, also a spiritual authority at the college, and he thought it an excellent idea.

So, with little comment and no fuss, Louis Jacobs was appointed moral tutor at Jews' College and took up his duties in 1960. He resigned his post at the New West End Synagogue and was succeeded as minister by the young and engaging Reverend Dr Chaim Pearl, whose theological views did not conflict with those Jacobs had propounded in his publications.

In 1961, Rabbi Dr Isidore Epstein retired as principal of Jews' College. Sir Alan Mocatta and the other lay officers of the college proposed that Louis Jacobs be appointed his successor, but Chief Rabbi Brodie vetoed the appointment. After much procrastination, he gave as his reasons, first, his objections to Jacobs's 'published views' and, secondly, that Jacobs did not possess the 'outstanding scholarship and other qualifications' required. That was the beginning of Jacobs Affair Part One. The more intense Part Two erupted in 1964.

With the veto on his appointment as principal, Louis resigned his post at the college and Sir Alan Mocatta and the other honorary officers resigned in sympathy. I had urged Louis Jacobs to stay on because I was convinced that, sooner or later, the appointment would come to him. There was no other obvious candidate for the principalship and the college could not go on long without leadership.

However, Louis felt that he had no other honourable course than resignation. A few 'Jacobites', led by former New West End congregant Ellis Franklin, formed the Society for the Study of Jewish Theology, with Louis as its director. That was intended as a stop-gap arrangement while Louis and his supporters worked out a long-term strategy.

In the meantime, I remained a congregant and friend of Chaim Pearl at the New West End. He did not find his appointment there fulfilling. He considered the membership staid and disinclined towards innovation. It was also elderly, giving few opportunities for as energetic an individual as he, and he occasionally confided his frustrations to me. In the course of our conversations, he often compared the New West End Synagogue unfavourably with the vigorous activity of the Conservative congregations of the United States. That gave me the thought of solving two problems at a stroke. If Chaim were to find a rewarding pulpit in America, he would be happier, and it would also leave a vacancy at the New West End to which Louis could return. I spoke about this to my friend Rabbi Wolfe Kelman, the executive head of the American Conservative Rabbinical Assembly, and as a result, Chaim was approached by a prestigious congregation just outside New York and he readily accepted a call to become its rabbi. The board of management of the New West End then unanimously invited Louis Jacobs to return to his former pulpit.

We were aware that the United Synagogue required the ministers of their constituent synagogues, before being appointed, to obtain a certificate from the Chief Rabbi that they were fit and proper persons for the job. Louis had received this certificate on his original appointment to the New West End and I had no doubt at the time that he would not be called upon to obtain another certificate: first, because he already possessed one; and second, because it would place the Chief Rabbi in another awkward situation I was sure he would rather avoid.

But I was wrong. Officialdom at the United Synagogue decreed that a new certificate was required, and it was intimated that, if Louis applied for one, it would not be granted. The synagogue board of management did not accept this ruling and formally appointed Jacobs to the post. Of

course, the United Synagogue could not accept this mutiny and
its secretary wrote to the wardens condemning the 'distinct
flouting' of the Chief Rabbi's authority and called on them to
'desist from taking any further action' and 'not permit Dr
Jacobs to officiate at the services of the synagogue'. The
synagogue board ignored this prohibition, and was thereupon
dismissed by resolution of the US authorities and replaced by
four 'managers'. As a result, the dismissed board and many
other congregants formed the New London Synagogue with
Louis as its rabbi.

The tumult and shouting over the Jacobs affairs, which
deeply divided Anglo-Jewry in the 1960s, undoubtedly provided
me with the most trying time of my editorship. I sided
wholeheartedly with Louis Jacobs but, while giving him the
fullest editorial support, I was acutely aware that, as a responsible newspaper, the *Jewish Chronicle* had to give the issue the
fullest and most objective coverage. The only snag about
presenting the anti-Jacobs case was that few were ready to write
articles setting it out, and that a great deal of the correspondence
on that side was either illiterate or simply vituperative.

Needless to say, we were given no credit for our efforts at
balanced reporting (as distinct from the editorials, which were
certainly partisan) and the paper and I were subject to much
vilification with the refrain, constantly repeated, that our
objective was solely to undermine Orthodoxy.

Brodie's heart was not in the fight and I was always
convinced that his views on revelation were no different from
the thesis of *We Have Reason to Believe* and that his virtual
excommunication of Jacobs was entirely due to his fear and
trembling before the Orthodox right wing, even though the
members of his court, the Beth Din, would have preferred to
see Louis back at the New West End.

For a long time, Brodie avoided any systematic explanation
of his objectives to Louis, but eventually it had to come and,
on 5 May 1964, he convened a meeting attended by 134 rabbis
and read a statement which included the following passage:

> The travesty of our traditional Judaism has been featured
> in our monopolistic Jewish press for some time. There
> has been a constant denigration of authentic Judaism and

religious authority which has tended to create religious confusion and a spirit of divisiveness within our community and which, in no small measure, has contributed to the present situation. Whilst we believe in the freedom of the press, we should not allow this freedom to be abused and even turned into a tyranny as is attempted by the Jewish Chronicle which, in recent years, no doubt for reasons of its own, has not presented an objective picture of the Anglo-Jewish scene, nor has it reflected the tradition and sentiment of Anglo-Jewry.

This ex-cathedra statement, reported fully in the *JC*, was read by the Chief Rabbi and no discussion was permitted. It pointedly refrained from according Louis the appellation of Rabbi, a surprising discourtesy to a recipient of the rabbinical diploma from the heads of the Manchester yeshivah and of the Manchester Beth Din, both institutions of unquestionable Orthodoxy. A voluminous postbag poured into the *JC*, of which we printed a representative selection. In a strongly worded editorial, I rebutted Dr Brodie's accusations. By that time, the controversy had become international news, with frequent reports and features in the British press as well as worldwide, with particularly extensive reporting in the *New York Times*. *The Economist*, in a leader, made the point that 'by vetoing Dr Jacobs's appointment at the New West End Synagogue, Dr Brodie appears to be taking up the illogical position that, while Dr Jacobs is fit to train future rabbis, he is not fit to be a rabbi himself'.

To some, I was the villain of the piece, abusing my office as editor to advance a personal cause and the career of a friend. In fact, nearly 80 years before my time, the *JC* had eloquently expressed the very cause which now constrained Chief Rabbi Brodie to denounce Louis Jacobs as a heretic. The *JC* issue of 5 March 1886 began with a leading article headed 'Judaism and Theology', which dealt with 'the position taken up by the old-fashioned school of theologians' that every word of the Bible is of directly divine origin. It argued that this has been proved to be untenable and the leader concluded: 'For if the religious and ethical ideas of the Jews are wonderful when regarded as the outcome of a direct communication from God to Man, they become still more marvellous viewed as the result of, so to speak, a partnership between the Deity and mortals.' Louis Jacobs could not have put it better.

Two rabbinical friends, one in the United States and the other in Israel, with whom I was in regular correspondence during this period, fortified me in my belligerence.

The Israeli was Rabbi Dr Louis Rabinowitz, a forceful spiritual leader who had, for many years, been the minister of the Cricklewood Synagogue, one of the more important constituents of the United Synagogue. Settling in Israel after his retirement, he remained a devoted reader of the *JC* and frequently favoured me with his advice and opinions on the contents of the paper.

He was what is now termed 'modern Orthodox' and would, in my opinion, have made an excellent Chief Rabbi after Brodie's retirement. But the hardliners ganged up on him and persuaded Sir Isaac Wolfson, then president of the US, that he was too old to be considered. He was then about 70 but full of physical and intellectual vigour and his appointment would certainly have halted the right-wing stranglehold on both the US and the Chief Rabbinate, but that was not to be.

During the second act of the Jacobs drama, Rabinowitz wrote to me from Jerusalem: 'The whole Orthodox intelligentsia in Israel agrees with me that Louis Jacobs was shamefully and cruelly treated.' He continued, 'a spirit of fanatical obscurantism has seized the whole official [Anglo-Jewish] community'.

Ultimately, this was a battle for the soul of Anglo-Jewry, between those advocating a free spirit of inquiry, as reinforcement to faith and tradition, and those who shunned reason out of blinkered, diehard, fundamentalism. Like most internecine battles, it generated much vehemence and acrimony. But I believe that the controversy did achieve the positive result of freshening the dormant waters of the Anglo-Jewish community, encouraging many of its members to face the challenge of reconciling tradition with modern knowledge.

I never thought that 'Jacobs II' could be won, for it was absolutely clear that the Chief Rabbi could not possibly be expected to rescind his veto. Sir Isaac Wolfson, the president of the United Synagogue, in a sense his employer, had tried to

persuade Dr Brodie that it would make sense to permit Louis
Jacobs to return to the New West End Synagogue. But Brodie
was not big enough to change direction and, in my case, was
totally intimidated by the Orthodox extremists. I fought the
battle because I believed I was serving the best interests of the
Jewish community and that, even though I could not win, it
might prepare the ground for a 'progressive conservative'
movement within traditional Anglo-Jewry.

It did. Immediately after the management of the New West
End Synagogue had been dismissed, its former wardens
convened a meeting of congregants. A large number attended
and a resolution was unanimously passed to form an
independent traditional congregation with the name of New
London Synagogue and with Louis Jacobs as its rabbi. Since we
had no premises, I asked the rabbinic leader of the Spanish &
Portuguese community, Haham Dr Solomon Gaon, if we could
use the hall of their Lauderdale Road Synagogue for Sabbath-
morning services and he readily agreed. The first service of the
new congregation took place before a packed and reverent
assembly and I think that my father, who had always wanted
me to be a cantor, would have been happy that I was asked to
lead it although he would probably have disapproved of the
New London's theology.

Our sojourn at Lauderdale Road was summarily cut short.
Dr Gaon told me that the acting Haham during his absence in
the United States, Rabbi Solomon Sassoon, whom I had known
in my childhood, had objected to this heretical activity on his
synagogue's premises. His opposition to the Jacobs
congregation could not be ignored. Gaon was unhappy about
having to withdraw his support but was unwilling to provoke
a split in his own community, which would undoubtedly have
occurred had the arrangement continued. Of course, I
understood his predicament and when I communicated his
message to the committee of the new synagogue, a hall in a
Kensington hotel was rented for its Sabbath services.

There we continued for some months while the leaders of
the congregation scouted around for permanent premises. One
Saturday evening, returning from the synagogue service, I
received a telephone call at home from Alec Colman, a well-
known and successful property man. He told me that, some

time ago, he had purchased the building of the St John's Wood Synagogue, a constituent of the United Synagogue, which was about to move to its new, spacious home. He had received planning permission to demolish the old building and replace it with a block of flats but, he told me, he felt very uncomfortable about pulling down a synagogue. Would we like to have it for the New London and, if so, he would sell it to us for the price he had paid?

I told him that I was sure it would be of interest and would inform my friends. He asked only one thing, and that was that his name should be kept out of it. He was a friend of Chief Rabbi Brodie and did not wish to have that relationship impaired. I assured him that his request would be honoured.

I consulted David Franklin, who had become the treasurer of the new congregation and was a personal friend. David was the eldest son of Ellis Franklin, the head of the distinguished Anglo-Jewish family, who had been one of Louis Jacobs's most loyal supporters. Without hesitation, David told me that he would find the money. Then followed some negotiation with Colman, who insisted that he should not be known as the seller to the heretics. I spoke to Louis Mintz, a friend and supporter of Louis who was also in the property business, and he agreed to purchase the property from Colman and then sell it to the New London Synagogue. That was duly executed and we were the owners of a stately old synagogue building on Abbey Road.

When the transaction became known and the building was being redecorated, a supporter of the Chief Rabbi entered it and removed the seat on which Brodie had sat whenever he attended this, his local synagogue. Those boards were never to be defiled by offering repose to the posterior of Louis Jacobs!

This Preface is an extract from William Frankel's memoir in progress and first appeared in the *Jewish Chronicle*, 26 September 2003.

CHAPTER I

Introduction

THERE are three pitfalls to be avoided by Jewish Apologetics in its attempt to grapple with the problems raised by modern thought. It must not refuse to recognise the existence of the problem by rejecting, in the name of tradition, modern thought and all its ways as of the devil. It must not encourage that division of the mind in which incompatible ideas are allowed to exist side by side in water-tight compartments. Nor must it be desperately stampeded into postulating an artificial synthesis, a queer hybrid faith which both the adherents of traditional Judaism and representative modern thinkers would repudiate. A true Jewish Apologetic, eschewing obscurantism, religious schizophrenia, and intellectual dishonesty, will be based on the conviction that all truth, 'the seal of the Holy One, blessed is He', is one, and that a synthesis is possible between the permanent values and truth of tradition and the best thought of the day.

The magnitude of the problem, the personal element involved in matters of faith, the fact that hardly anybody, nowadays, is thoroughly at home in both modern philosophy and the massive Jewish learning of the past, the many subjects to be mastered before Jewish religious philosophy can be presented as an organic, life-embracing whole, the nature of the investigation as an encounter with the mysterious and unfathomable, all these combine to make pretentious and hollow the claim that an easy solution has been found.

'So far as concerns religious problems, simple solutions are bogus solutions. It is written that he who runs may read. But it is not said that he provides the writing' (Whitehead). But it remains true that every religious person aware of the problem has some kind of working solution, albeit a tentative one, and this book is offered in the hope that the views expressed may be of some interest to others treading the same path.

9

It cannot be denied that theology, especially dogmatic theology, is viewed with suspicion; as a wit has said: 'Any stigma is good enough to beat the dogma'. And since the days of Moses Mendelssohn (1729–1786) there has been much discussion on the place of dogma in Judaism. But while it is true that Judaism is far less dogmatic than Christianity, with its beliefs less rigidly defined so that there is greater scope for individual interpretation, thinking Jews and Jewesses are no longer satisfied with a faith that in Schechter's phrase is 'all things to all men'. Thouless,[1] discussing the expression 'fettered by outworn creeds' rightly says: 'This metaphor is also objectionable in the implications of the word "outworn". Some things (such as knives and other physical implements) become increasingly unserviceable as they grow older; other things (such as the multiplication table) do not. There is no necessity for supposing that dogmas belong to the first class rather than the second. If a true assertion was made many centuries ago, there is no gain in replacing it by a false statement made more recently. No reverence for antiquity must make us hesitate to discard an old statement if we have good reason for thinking it is false. But the question is one of truth or falsity, not of age as is implied by the use of the word "outworn".' Jews today are interested in theological questions. Religious Jews want to be sure that their faith is no vague emotion but is grounded in reality. They want to be in the position of confidently asserting: 'We have *reason* to believe'.

A few years ago, *The Jewish Chronicle* published, under the title 'The Persistent Questioner', a series of articles by young writers on the problems of faith.[2] The two most significant features of this symposium were that, with one exception, the writers argued in favour of the traditional form of Judaism and that more than one made it clear that orthodoxy need not be equated with fundamentalism. These points are worth considering. The riches of traditional Judaism have the power to grip the imagination, but, for the results to be lasting, tradition must speak in the language of the day and its teachings must not run counter to established truth. Much attention

[1] *Authority and Freedom*, Lond., 1954, p. 30.
[2] *The Jewish Chronicle*, Oct., 1953–Jan., 1954.

has been focused on the question of fundamentalism by the astonishing successes of the Christian evangelist, Billy Graham. When this dynamic preacher of a naïve faith was invited to address a student body in Cambridge, *The Times* published letters from prominent Churchmen, among others, deploring his fundamentalist approach which, successful though it is, fails to take note of the researches of sound Biblical scholarship. Jews have much to learn from all this. The proud Jewish claim that loyalty to Judaism involves no surrender of the Jew's reasoning powers can be substantiated if present-day problems of belief are faced with the same blend of respect for reason and reverence for tradition that was so marked a feature of the approach of the great mediaeval thinkers—Saadiah, Ibn Ezra, Maimonides and Crescas.

In the following pages the three pillars on which traditional Judaism rests—the belief in God, in His Torah and in the rôle of Israel as His people—are examined with special reference to the difficulties raised by modern thought. This theme has, of course, been dealt with before—Dr. Epstein's 'The Faith of Judaism' contains the most recent treatment—but the works on it are so few in number that a 'professional' Rabbi who often has occasion to discuss these topics, may be forgiven for adding his contribution to the discussion. Chapter II contrasts the traditional idea of God with its latter-day rival in terms of 'process'. Chapters III and IV deal with the reasons for believing in God's existence and the argument that religious belief is an illusion. The problem of why a benevolent God tolerates pain and suffering, the most stubborn obstacle to Theistic faith, is considered in Chapter V. The next four chapters deal with the concept of Torah and the challenge presented by critical studies into Jewish origins. Arising out of this, the Jewish attitude towards miracles is examined in Chapter X. The last chapter deals with the Chosen People idea and the unique character of Judaism. But Judaism has an other-worldly as well as a this-worldly approach to the religious life so that a preliminary chapter on the After-life is not out of place.

There are obvious omissions. Many more theological topics are both interesting and relevant to modern man's predicament. But the aim of this book has not been to attempt a survey of the whole field. Its concern is with attitude and mood rather than with a detailed presentation of Jewish Theology. If it stimulates its readers to think seriously about their faith and even helps some of them to declare 'We have reason to believe' this will be its justification.

CHAPTER II

What is Meant by God?

GOD is thought of in many different ways; it may be that there are as many conceptions of God as there are human beings. For some, God is a stern patriarchal Being, surveying the world He has created like a king presiding over the destinies of His people. For others, He is best described as a benevolent Father, viewing with compassion the deeds of His creatures, loving them for their virtues and full of pity for their waywardness, sin and stupidity. For others again, the God-concept is degraded unless it is conveyed by such non-human terms as 'Force' or 'Power' or 'First Cause'. 'The general English view of God', said Tennyson, 'is as of an immeasurable clergyman, and some mistake the devil for God'. Yet a religious genius, the mediaeval thinker and poet, Solomon Ibn Gabirol, could say that though men conceive of God in different ways and worship Him in their own fashion, they are all groping for the same truth. From the savage prostrating himself before his totem pole to the philosopher searching for Ultimate Reality, the object of all their striving is One. As the author of the Jewish 'Hymn of Glory' puts it:

> They told of Thee, but not as Thou must be,
> Since from Thy work they tried to body Thee.
> To countless visions did their picture run,
> Behold through all the visions Thou art one.

Far from religion having any quarrel with the idea of God's incomprehensibility, all higher religious teaching is unanimous in insisting that God can only be known through His deeds, never as He is in Himself. The book of Exodus thus records Moses' request to be shown God's glory:

> Thou canst not see My face, for man shall not see Me and live! And the Lord said: 'Behold there is a place by

Me, and thou shalt stand upon the rock. And it shall come to pass, while My glory passeth by, that I will put thee in a cleft of the rock, and will cover thee with My hand until I have passed by. And I will take away My hand, and thou shalt see My back; but My face shall not be seen'.[1]

God cannot be *defined* for definition is *genus* plus *differentia*. If, for example, man is defined as a rational creature, there is first the statement of the *genus*—the group to which he belongs—and then the statement of how he differs from other members of that group. We say that man is a member of the group 'creatures' and that by possessing reasoning faculties he differs from all other members of that group. But on any advanced view of Theism, God cannot belong to a group, for this would imply that the group to which He belongs is greater, i.e. more embracing than He. The Kabbalists in their eagerness to emphasize God's incomprehensibility go so far as to speak of Him as *'Ayin*—He Who is Not—that is to say one cannot, strictly speaking, even say that God *exists*, for this, too, is an attempted description of that which cannot be described.

It is because of the difficulty involved in speaking of God—a difficulty inseparable from the belief in an Infinite Being far beyond the uttermost reaches of the finite human mind (Moses, said a Hasidic teacher, is described as 'slow of speech'[2] because the more a man knows of God the more incapable he is of expressing what he knows)—that human beings fall into one of two errors when so speaking: that of *anthropomorphism*, of describing God in human terms, or the opposite error of describing Him as an impersonal Power to which no kind of consciousness can be ascribed. Either view is inconsonant with the true Theistic position.

To examine anthropomorphism first. In the classical Jewish writings, when human qualities are hesitatingly attributed to God, because this is the only way in which humans can speak of the Highest (as Schechter says: 'Judaism never objected to ascribing human qualities to God, but only to ascribing divine qualities to man'), attention is generally called to the inade-

[1] Ex. xxxiii. 20–23.
[2] Ex. iv. 10.

quacy of the description by the word *kebheyakhol*, meaning 'as if it were possible'. Maimonides (1135–1204), the greatest Jewish thinker of the Middle Ages, in his Code of Jewish law, goes so far as to teach that he who entertains anthropomorphic notions of Deity, believing that God can actually be described in human terms, is a heretic and has no share in the life to come.[1] Abraham Ibn David of Posquieres (c. 1125–1198), the critic of Maimonides, whose pungent strictures on the latter's views range over the whole field covered by the Code, refuses to follow him here, arguing that it is unreasonable to treat the Jew who entertains cruder notions as a heretic, for not everyone is capable of grasping the fact that the anthropomorphic Biblical and Rabbinic passages are not to be taken literally. But, in principle, Ibn David agrees that, ideally, only the refined conception is permissible. The metaphorical language used by religion has been compared to a map. A map is not a picture, it contains symbolic representation, e.g. two curved lines for a bridge, but because of this it is the more helpful. We must not, however, fall into the error of treating it as a picture.[2]

Maimonides, developing this theme, goes on to say that one can only ascribe to God *negative* attributes, i.e. one can only say what God is *not*, never what He *is*. In this view, to say that He is merciful can only mean that He is not cruel, to say that He is true is only to say that He is not false. Even to say that He is *One* is not to *describe* Him or to make any positive assertion about His nature, but simply to deny that there is a plurality of gods. Or even to say that He exists is merely to deny that He is non-existent. Such negative descriptions have value, however, for the more we know about what God is not the nearer we are to the knowledge of Him as He is, though this knowledge can never be fully comprehended by man. If, for instance, we wish to describe the occupant of a house by means of negative attributes, we can first say that what is in the house is not an inanimate thing. We now know a little more about the occupant, though nothing positive has been said about him. If we then go on to say that the occupant

[1] Yad. Hil. Tesh. III. 7.
[2] Robert H. Thouless, *op. cit.* p. 64.

is not a bird, not a non-human animal and so on, with each 'negative qualification' a little more is known.[1]

Some moderns, recognising the absurdity of anthropomorphism, go to the opposite extreme, refusing to speak of a 'Personal' God, i.e. a Being possessing Mind and Consciousness. The mistake here is to imagine that because God cannot be described in human terms it is preferable to equate the Ground of reality with some non-human 'Force' or 'Process', whereas in the Theistic view it is at least as false to describe God in non-human as in human terms. God can only be addressed as God ('I am that I am')[2] though no human being can so address Him. Admittedly, God cannot be described by humans but if we are to speak of Him at all we must perforce use the highest terms we know to do that work, always with the mental reservation that He is more than that which we are saying He is. To speak of God as 'Power' or 'Force' or 'Process', without reference to mind or will, is to make Him less than we are ourselves for we do possess minds and wills and consciousness. If we follow Maimonides, we would say that by a *Personal* God is meant a Being Who is not *non-Personal*, Who is not inert to our prayers, our worship and our endeavours to seek Him. In the words of a modern writer on religion, God is a *He*, not an *It*; or perhaps it would be better to say that He is both a *He* and an *It*; He is, that is to say, *more* than personality, not *less*.[3]

This whole question is worthy of note for there is a school of thought in modern Jewish life which professes to find much meaning in Judaism and which even advocates Jewish observance in the traditional sense but which has denuded the God concept of its *Personal* element. The Reconstructionist School —the leader of which is the distinguished American Jewish thinker, Mordecai Kaplan—has contributed much to the revaluation of Judaism in the light of twentieth century life and thought. Its ideas, particularly in the sociological field, are generally stimulating and frequently significant. The writings of its members have acted as a useful corrective to the substi-

---

[1] Guide, Part I, 57–60.
[2] Ex. iii. 14.
[3] Will Herberg: *Judaism and Modern Man*, N.Y., 1952, p. 60f.

tution of rhetoric for reason and enthusiasm for conviction. But its claim to 're-interpret' the God idea in non-personal terms is the most radical departure from the Jewish-Theistic view ever undertaken by those who have remained 'within the fold'. The claim made by this school is that the traditional conception of God is no longer tenable;[1] that for modern man God must be defined as 'the Power that makes for salvation'.

Kaplan, in his book *The Meaning of God in Modern Jewish Religion*, develops the thesis that modern man cannot conceive of God as a 'Person' but as the relationships, tendencies and agencies which in their totality go to make human life worthwhile in the deepest and most abiding sense. Religion can no longer be a matter of entering into relationship with the supernatural. Godhood can have no meaning for modern man apart from human ideals of truth, goodness, and beauty, interwoven in a pattern of holiness.[2] Thus, says Kaplan, 'to believe in God is to reckon with life's creative forces, tendencies and potentialities as forming an organic unity, and as giving meaning to life by virtue of that unity'.[3] This means that we have faith that reality is so constituted as to enable man to achieve salvation. If it be asked how we know that reality is so constituted, Kaplan would reply that this is where faith comes in, that the human mind cannot find rest until it finds order in the universe, that the human personality must affirm that human life is supremely worthwhile.[4]

On the basis of these thoughts Kaplan is able to conclude: 'Belief in God as here conceived can function in our day exactly as the belief in God has always functioned; it can function as an affirmation that life has value. It implies, as the God idea has always implied, a certain assumption with regard to the nature of reality, the assumption that reality is so constituted as to endorse and guarantee the realisation in man of that which is of greatest value to him. If we believe that assumption to be true, for it is an assumption that is not sus-

---

[1] Though it is only fair to point out that the Reconstructionist School does not claim that there is only one conception of God and some of its members disagree with Kaplan's non-personal conception.

[2] *The Meaning of God in Modern Jewish Religion*, N.Y., 1937, p. 25–6.

[3] *Ibid.*, p. 26.

[4] *Ibid.*, p. 27.

ceptible of proof, we have faith in God. No metaphysical speculation beyond this fundamental assumption that reality assures both the emergence and the realisation of human ideals is necessary for the religious life'.[1]

Again and again Kaplan returns to the attack, zealously supported by his disciples. And the burden of their contention is always the same: that to ascribe 'personality' to God is to commit the anthropomorphic fallacy. Ira Eisenstein, a leader of the Reconstructionist movement, writes: 'In the patriarchal age they used to think that God would appear to this one or that one in dreams and visions. Later on, they believed that God revealed Himself once, and once only, to the whole people on Mt. Sinai. Still later, they believed that God had transmitted an unwritten tradition that was equally His word. In the philosophic age they used to believe that God was not to be defined except in negatives. He became a kind of philosophic principle. To the cabalists He was a sort of object of magic. To the *Hasidim* He was a sort of jolly father, kindly and protective. To the mystics He was one thing; to the rationalists He was another; and modern Jewish philosophies have a score of different conceptions of God.'[2] Eisenstein concludes, therefore, that a distinction must be drawn between the *belief* in God and the *conception* of God. Conceptions of God differ, belief in God must be constant in Judaism. So far we can follow him. But he then goes on to argue that if *conceptions* differ there is no reason for denying the validity of the 'Reconstructionist' conception. 'Belief in God (writes Eisenstein) I think we must all have, because belief in God, in the final analysis, means believing in two things—believing that the ideals we cherish are real, that such things as justice and peace and brotherhood and mercy and compassion and honesty are not merely convenient arrangements which society somehow works out, but that these actually correspond to the very structure of the universe. This is the way the universe was put together. To believe in God means to believe in the reality of these spiritual ideals. To believe in God means,

[1] *Ibid.*, p. 29.
[2] *My Philosophy of Judaism* in *The Reconstructionist*, Vol. XXI, April 15, 1955, p. 9.

secondly, to have faith that these ideals can win out in the end. It means believing that no matter what obstacles, no matter what discouragements we may face, eventually, these ideals are bound to be realised, if we work and continue to inspire one another.'[1]

Herein lies the distinction between the traditional Theistic view and the 'Reconstructionist'. For the traditional Theist, the ideals of which Eisenstein speaks are real and they will win out in the end *because* God exists. For Eisenstein and those who think like him, the conclusion appears to be that the ideals themselves and the process of 'winning out' are God and nothing *more* is God. And this conclusion is entirely unwarranted by the evidence he adduces that in the past men held different *conceptions* of God. For Eisenstein's is not merely a different conception of the same thing. It differs from all the others not alone in degree but in kind. It omits that which all the other conceptions share, the belief in God's 'personality', or better, God's *super-personality*. Eisenstein would certainly repudiate the view that cruelty, hatred and war are God and that these will ultimately 'win out'—this was, in fact, the view of Hitler. But on what grounds would such a repudiation be based if not that you cannot call *anything* God without doing violence to the normal canons of speech? So that the question does reduce itself, as Eisenstein recognises, to what did religious people mean when they spoke of God. And it is incorrect to suggest that they meant only the ideals Eisenstein mentions and the process of 'winning out'. They did mean this but it must be obvious that, in addition, they meant, and still do mean, the concept of 'personality'.

Kaplan himself, in a reply to the question: 'Does Reconstructionism offer an adequate God idea?' remarks: 'All the theologians who deprecate the naïve conception of God as an anthropomorphic being, virtually do not themselves believe in God as an identifiable being or entity. When they denounce the notion of God as Process, they apparently try to convey the impression that their own idea of God is at least comprehensible. Actually, they keep on stressing at the same time that God is absolutely unknowable, inscrutable, and ineffable.

[1] *The Reconstructionist, ibid.*

They use the very terms in which the agnostic Herbert Spencer long ago described God. They keep on repeating that we can know God only through his manifestations, or that He reveals Himself not in objects but in events. What are manifestations and events, if not process? These theologians are merely hurling at the notion of God as Process the same anathemas that have been hurled at the God idea of the mediaeval theologians by the naïve pietists who conceived of God in human form.'[1] But has Kaplan successfully identified his 'refined' concept with the statement of the theologians that we can only know God through His manifestations or through events? What are manifestations or events if not process, Kaplan asks? To which the obvious answer is that they are 'process' but for the theologians God is *revealed* through process whereas for Kaplan God *is* process. No theologian worthy of the name would try to do what Kaplan accuses him of doing; i.e. to prove that his idea of God is comprehensible. The theologian is concerned to demonstrate, that the idea of an incomprehensible God is comprehensible! 'We can apprehend, but cannot comprehend God' (Von Hügel).

Throughout Kaplan's writings—and no one would wish to deny the profundity of his thought and the many stimulating ideas his works contain—there is the tacit assumption that our increased knowledge compels us to give up the traditional God idea and that the only honest intellectual alternative to out-and-out atheism is a re-interpretation of that idea in the terms of Reconstructionism. It is no accident that the word 'naïve' occurs twice in the passage quoted above.

Kaplan, in the article just quoted, goes on to argue: 'The complaint of those who assail the view of God as the Power that makes for salvation is virtually a restatement in somewhat more modern terms, of Moses Taku's insistence that only the belief in the corporeality of God is in line with genuine Jewish doctrine, and of his denunciation of Maimonides as an arch-heretic. Shall we learn nothing from the anti-Maimonist controversy? Does it not prove beyond a shadow of a doubt that so long as a conception of God is compatible with prayer and worship, it is legitimate? To be sure, a conception of God

may meet this requirement, and yet not be compatible with
the traditional belief in the *theurgic* effect of prayer. As far as
that is concerned, it is doubtful whether most of the contemporary existentialist conceptions of God, like those of
Rosenzweig, Buber or Niebuhr, would go so far as to imply
that prayer can be a means of ending a drought, or that it can
cure cancer and pneumonia'.

Leaving aside the somewhat cavalier dismissal of the validity
of petitionary prayer,[1] let us accept Kaplan's definition of a
valid 'Jewish' conception of God—as one compatible with
prayer and worship. This is precisely the point. Is Kaplan's
conception compatible with prayer and worship? Can you
worship a Process? Reconstructionists would answer that you
can and it would be gratuitously insulting to imply that they
are deluding themselves when they do worship this 'impersonal'
Power. But we are entitled to say that those who cannot
accept the Reconstructionist conception find it impossible to
understand how anyone can *worship* an impersonal force,
which, precisely because it lacks personality, is less than the
worshipper himself. As Chesterton, criticising the apotheosis
of the Life Force, said: 'You cannot worship a cypher'!

This question is a fundamental one. It cuts right across the
usual religious divisions in Jewry. There are Jews subscribing
to the Reconstructionist philosophy, who keep many of the
practical observances of Judaism—as 'folk-ways'—and there
are, on the other hand, many Reform Jews who keep very
little of traditional Jewish ritual who would emphatically reject the 'non-Personal' conception of God. As a Reform Rabbi
recently put it: 'While Classical Reform was eating *terefah*
and thinking *kasher*, Reconstructionists eat *kasher* and think
terefah.' Bernard J. Heller is justified in saying: 'The prover-
bial prayer, "God protect me from my friends, I'll take care of
my enemies", could well describe the attitude of the Jewish
religionists to the so-called Jewish humanists of the lay, and
more so of the rabbinical, variety. We need not fear the
atheist and sceptic. He has adopted a philosophy and has taken
a definite position. He tells people unequivocally what he

---

[1] For a brief discussion of this see my little book *Jewish Prayer*, Lond.,
1962, p. 8f.

believes or disbelieves and where he stands. He calls a spade a spade. This makes it easy for us to comprehend his views and appraise them and point out what seems to us their inadequacies. It is, however, not so with the Jewish humanists. They vacillate and equivocate. They negate the cardinal affirmations and attitude which religion demands or implies, and yet they persist in using the term God. They propound the tenets of secular ethicism, but yet they insist on doing so from the pulpits of synagogues. When this dichotomy is called to their attention, they retort that they are re-interpreting old concepts by pouring new wine in old bottles. They forget that such procedure is legitimate when the essence and nature of the new and old are more alike than they are different. It is *all right to pour new wine into old bottles, but it is certainly improper to pour vinegar into receptacles that were wont to contain champagne*.[1]

To sum up: the best Jewish thinkers, mystics, saints and scholars have tried to avoid, when thinking of God, the extremes of both anthropomorphism and 'de-personalisation'. God as apprehended in traditional Judaism is the Supreme Being, Who is known through His deeds, never comprehended as He is in Himself, Who is more than personality not less, and Who, because this is so, can be worshipped by His creatures who will find Him if they seek Him.

[1] *The Modernist's Revolt Against God*, Proceedings of the Central Conference of American Rabbis, Vol. XL, 1930.

CHAPTER III

The Proof of God's Existence

DURING the Biblical and Rabbinic periods no attempts were made to prove the existence of God. This was taken for granted; the ancients appear never to have entertained doubts on this question. The Bible knows of the sceptic (witness the books of Ecclesiastes and Job); there are many references, in the Talmudic literature, to heretics, but these appear to have been men who doubted God's providence, or some other aspect of the faith commonly held, not those who doubted the very existence of God. Even the verse in Psalms: 'The fool hath said in his heart: "There is no God" '[1] means not so much a denial of God's existence as that He intervenes in human affairs. The same applies to the Rabbinic *kopher ba-'ikar*—'he who denies the root principle' —as the frequently quoted Rabbinic equivalent 'there is no judge and no judgment' shows.

When the Midrash describes Abraham's recognition of his Creator, it gives the illustration of a man walking on his way at night who saw a mansion on fire and concluded that the mansion had no owner, until the owner of the mansion looked out at him and said: 'I am the owner of this mansion'.[2] That is, the lack of justice in the world frequently leads men to conclude that God is not concerned with human affairs, as the burning mansion leads one to conclude that there is no one to care for it *now*, no *owner*. But the implication is that no one could have doubted that it had, in the first place, a *builder*, who put it where it stands. As Robert Gordis says of Ecclesiastes:[3] 'The modern reader might expect that Koheleth would be led by his views to deny the existence of God, but that was impossible to an ancient mind, and especially to a

[1] Ps. xiv. 1.
[2] B.R. 39, 1.
[3] *Koheleth—The Man and His World*, N.Y., 1955, p. 112.

23

Jew. Even the Epicureans who denied the gods' intervention in human affairs as a fundamental element of their outlook, did not deny their being. In the ancient world, atheism, the denial of God, referred to the view that the gods do not intervene in the human affairs. Koheleth, a son of Israel, reared on the words of the Torah, the Prophets and the Sages, could not doubt the reality of God for an instant. For him, the existence of the world was tantamount to the existence of God'. In the classical statement on those who have no share in the life to come, the Rabbis speak of those who deny the resurrection of the dead or the divine origin of the Torah[1] but the atheist is not mentioned because he was virtually unknown in Rabbinic times.

It was under the impact of Greek philosophy that Jews were impelled to adduce proofs of God's existence. Philo of Alexandria and religious thinkers in the Middle Ages—Moslem and Christian as well as Jewish—claimed that man could arrive at belief in God by the use of his own unaided reason. The following are the three main philosophical proofs, found especially in the writings of the mediaeval theologians:

(a) the *cosmological*—every cause can be traced to an earlier cause, but what is the origin of the first cause? This First Cause must be a Being Who exists without a cause and this is God.

(b) the *ontological*—the notion in the human mind of a Perfect Being implies that He exists for if He did not exist He would not be perfect. This appears to be merely playing with words. Whatever force the argument has it derives from the difficulty of accounting for the idea of God in the human mind. If God does not exist how did human beings come to think of Him?

(c) the *teleological*—the argument from design. There is evidence of design in the universe, i.e. in the patterns of the leaf, the structure of the human body—there are millions of cells in the human brain, for example, all knit together in one system and working in co-ordination—in the growth of plant and animal life, the movement of the planets, and

[1] Sanh, x. 1.

the workings of the human mind. But there can be no design without a mind, so that evidence of design in the universe is evidence of a Designer, Who is God. Both the cosmological and teleological arguments are found in the works of the mediaeval Jewish thinkers; the ontological argument, invented by St. Anselm was either unknown or unacceptable to them, for it appears nowhere in their works.

Since Kant, these proofs have been heavily assailed. The *cosmological* proof is held to be inadequate because it does not really explain that which it sets out to do. The difficulty of how the first cause came into being is no less if God is postulated as that Cause. Little children, with the perspicacity of innocence, often ask: 'Who made God?' The *ontological* proof is unsound because it is possible for the human mind to have in it the idea of a mythical creature such as a unicorn or a griffon, and no one would argue that because of this these creatures must actually exist. Finally, the *teleological* proof is attacked on the grounds that the evidence from design is ambiguous; if design is used as proof of the existence of a Supremely Good and Omnipotent Being, what of faulty or even positively evil design evident in the universe? For if design is manifest in the intricate, beautiful patterns of the leaf and flower it can be seen, too, in the devourng cancerous growth; and the human eye, wonderful though it is, is an imperfect instrument for a divine artificer to have fashioned.

Many theologians, nowadays, accept the validity of these refutations and admit that there can be no proof of God in the sense that there can be proof of a mathematical formula (we have seen that the ancient Hebrews did not believe in God because they had arrived at His existence by speculation). But they go on to remark that we can be convinced of a thing beyond a shadow of doubt by means other than that of mathematical proof. There is no such proof, for instance, of the existence of other human beings beside ourselves, yet we are convinced that they do exist.

> Thou canst not prove the Nameless, O my son,
> Nor canst thou prove the world thou movest in,
> Thou canst not prove that thou art body alone,

Nor canst thou prove that thou art spirit alone,
Nor canst thou prove that thou art both in one:
Thou canst not prove that thou art immortal, no,
Nor yet that thou art mortal—nay, my son,
Thou canst not prove that I, who speak with thee,
Am not thyself in converse with thyself,
For nothing worthy proving can be proven,
Nor yet disproven.

(*Tennyson.*)

In the nature of the case, the evidence of the senses cannot demonstrate the existence of that which is not of the senses, nor can the effort of the human intellect demonstrate the existence of that which is more than human intellect. To say this is not to surrender reason—this would be suicidal, for unreliable as the human reason may be it is the only instrument we have for testing truth—but a recognition, in the name of reason itself, that we must look beyond it for the apprehension of certain truths. In other words a distinction must be drawn between *proof* and *conviction*—proof is one of the ways to conviction but there are other ways, too. So that the real question is not whether the existence of God can be proven but whether belief in His existence is overwhelmingly convincing.

Many have arrived at this conviction as the result of a personal experience which convinces them that God exists. These men would rule out of court the very discussion of whether God exists, for, they would say, if a man is truly in love he does not ask himself if he is in love. The *experience* of God's Presence is sufficient. This is the mystical approach to religion, the approach of the Besht, founder of the Hasidic movement, who was fond of quoting the verse: 'Taste ye and see that the Lord is good'.[1] Religious experience, he said, is compared to tasting food—the taste cannot be conveyed, it must be experienced. The Hasidim tell of one of their leaders who once startled his followers sitting with him at table, by asking them: 'Do you believe in God?' 'Rabbi,' was their horrified reply, 'of course we believe in God.' 'Well I do not,' said the Rabbi.

[1] Psalms xxxiv. 9.

And he went on to explain: 'Do you *believe* that we are sitting at a table? You *know* that we are sitting at a table.' It is said that in one of the African dialects, deficient in names for abstract ideas, the nearest to the word 'believe' is 'to hear in the heart'!

But this approach cannot be of much help to one who has never had an experience of this nature, though there is valuable evidence for the truth of the religious hypothesis in the remarkable unanimity in which those who claim to have had mystical experience record that experience. The mystics of quite different ages and climes all seem to have 'seen' the same vision. And very many people, far removed from the conventional picture of the mystic, claim to have had a similar experience, claim to 'know' that God exists.

In recent years the religious Existentialist movement has won many adherents. This movement considers the attempt to prove the existence of God an impertinence. God must be *encountered*. We cannot calmly discuss whether God exists as if we were debating an intellectual puzzle which has no relevance to our lives. If we are to experience religious truth we must take what Kierkegaard calls 'the leap of faith', we must respond with our whole being to the call of God, we must be personally committed, and only then will God reveal Himself to us. The Jewish existentialist approach can be studied especially in the works of Martin Buber and Franz Rosenzweig and their disciples.[1]

Many religious thinkers, on the other hand, still favour the 'rational' approach to religious belief, convinced that the final word has not been said on this subject by the Kantians. Kant himself was convinced of God's existence because of the prickings of conscience—the 'voice of God'—in the human breast. In an oft-quoted passage Kant remarks: 'Two things fill the mind with ever-increasing wonder and awe, the more often and the more intensely the mind of thought is drawn to them: the starry heavens above me and the moral law within me'.

[1] For Buber and Rosenzweig see; Jacob B. Agus: *Modern Philosophies of Judaism*, N.Y., 1941, Nahum N. Glatzer: *Franz Rosenzweig*, N.Y., 1953, Will Herberg: *Judaism and Modern Man*, N.Y., 1951. Maurice S. Friedman: Martin Buber, *The Life of Dialogue*, Lond., 1955. 'Martin Buber—Jewish Existentialist' by Malcolm Diamond, N.Y., 1960.

The late Chief Rabbi of Palestine, Rav Kook, one of the profoundest modern Jewish religious thinkers, went so far as to say that obedience to the moral law was itself obedience to God even if not recognised as such. Thus he remarked that the religious person ought not to feel disturbed or dismayed when he sees people without any kind of religious affiliation working for social justice, for these men are 'doing God's work without knowing it' ('Letters': No. 44).

The point is also worthy of note that the urge to worship in the human breast affords evidence of God's existence. 'Man must worship something; if he does not worship God, he will worship an idol made of wood or of gold or of ideas' (Dostoievsky).

Other thinkers, again, hold that though each of the traditional proofs in itself is unconvincing, taken together they are convincing. For the Kantian objections are not complete refutations of the proofs. They do no more than demonstrate the weakness of each of them taken by itself. Granted that the proofs carry no weight as *evidence*, they are *indications* and as such have the power of supplementing each other.

Catholic thinkers in particular attach great importance to the traditional proofs and while Judaism is, of course, not committed to the view that God's existence can be proven in this way, Jews have tended to attach importance to the argument from design in particular. The story is told of some sages from a distant land who, hearing of the fame of Maimonides, came to him with a request that he prove to them that God exists. Maimonides, the legend has it, left them in his room, on the table of which there was a beautifully written manuscript full of the profoundest thoughts. On his return the philosopher was asked who wrote the manuscript. 'The ink pot just happened to topple over and it wrote itself' was his reply. 'But that is absurd.' 'Exactly, and this is the answer to your query!' There is, it cannot be denied, evidence of evil or badly-conceived design but the Theistic position is not that the universe is perfect, but that its Creator is perfect. It might be asked why a perfect Creator should have created an imperfect universe; then we are face to face with the problem of evil—admittedly the most stubborn obstacle in the path of faith. In a later chapter some of the thoughts that have been expressed on this problem will be noted but for our purpose it is sufficient to say that evidence for design there is and design implies a Mind. To say that that Mind is evil leaves unexplained the evidence of good and benevolent design. To postulate the existence of *two* Minds—the one good, the other evil—is to restate the Zoroastrian belief in Ormuzd and Ahriman, a belief we feel instinctively to be false. 'That they may know from the rising of the sun, and from the west, That there is none beside Me; I am the Lord, and there is none else; I form the light, and create darkness; I make peace and create evil; I am the Lord, that doeth all these things'.[1]

And while the cosmological proof offers no conclusive argument for God's existence it reminds us that the alternative is to give no rational explanation of the world at all but just to accept it. If we think about it we do find it incredible to believe that the universe just happened.[2]

There is finally, the evidence of heroic men and women whose lives have been transformed and ennobled because of their belief in God. We cannot describe electricity, no one knows what it is, but we can observe its effects, we know that it provides us with light and warmth. It is true that men have committed abominations in the name of religion but some of the greatest men who ever lived, some of the greatest benefactors of the human race, have been inspired and guided by their religious faith.

What it all amounts to is this, that while the existence of God cannot be proved if we start from the beginning, none of us do, in fact, start from the beginning. We are presented with two alternative beliefs about ultimate reality and we have to choose between them. According to one view God exists—it is He Who created us, Who fashioned our minds and implanted the moral sense within us so that we are capable of recognising beauty, truth and goodness and fighting ugliness, falsehood and evil. In this view the difficulty is how to account

[1] Isaiah xlv. 6–7.
[2] A splendid, readable account of the value of the cosmological and teleological arguments is given in the chapter on God in A. C. Ewing's: *The Fundamental Questions of Philosophy*, Lond., 1951.

for the existence of evil. According to the other view there is no God. Religious people who believe in Him are deluding themselves, their invention of 'arguments' to prove His existence is a subtle kind of wish-fulfilment. In this view the difficulties are how mind came from matter, how life emerged where there was no life before, how the universe itself came into being, how the good is possible of realisation and how man came to strive for it—how man as a tiny part of the universe came to pass judgment on it? Difficulties there are in both views but the believer is convinced that his view is the only one that makes any kind of sense of the universe. A modern convert to Theism from atheism has summed up the matter thus: 'If, so far as your reason takes you, the religious view of the universe seems to afford the most plausible explanation of your experience, then it seems not unreasonable to follow this same view at which it leaves reason behind. If it accounts for the things you know and can understand, then it seems to me not unreasonable to hold that it could also offer an explanation of the things that you do not know and cannot possibly understand—always, of course, provided that it is not positively at variance with the findings of any aspect of your experience and does not positively contradict the conclusions of reason in regard to the things that you do believe yourself to know.'[1]

The truth of the matter is that there are two approaches to God, not contradictory but complementary. These are expressed in the words of the triumphant song of victory the Israelites sang at the shores of the Red Sea when, with the miseries of their past behind them and the promised land in front, they found God.

> This is my God, and I will glorify Him;
> My father's God, and I will exalt him.[2]

Judaism emphasizes both the concept 'God of the fathers' and the need for personal religious experience expressed in the concept 'my God'.

The concept 'God of the fathers' cannot in itself provide a

[1] C. S. Joad: *The Recovery of Belief*, Lond., 1952, p. 19.
[2] Ex. xv. 2.

sufficient or permanent basis for the life of faith. 'You cannot worship God,' said Schechter, 'with your father's heart.' There comes a time when the ancestral faith becomes meaningless unless it finds its response in the depths of the individual soul. One of the great Jewish moralists of the last century said that the devout Jew speaks, in his prayers, of the '*God* of Abraham, the *God* of Isaac, the *God* of Jacob' not the 'God of Abraham, Isaac and Jacob,' because each of the Patriarchs discovered God for himself. God was not the God of Isaac simply because He was the God of his father, nor was He the God of Jacob simply because He was the God of his father and grandfather. Most people appear to have known the kind of intuition that comes to us with a sense of overwhelming clarity in the rare moments of intense religious experience and moral fervour when we know that righteousness has an objective reality, when we know that God exists. It is this kind of experience— too real to be dismissed as an illusion, too intimate to be discussed fully with others—that gives faith its conviction. Once a person has known this, once he has known what it means to say: 'my God', all argument on the question of God's existence seems to him to be so much logic chopping. (This is not, of course, to deny that there is an ebb and flow in the life of faith. The Hasidim, for example, spoke of the states of *gadluth demohin*—'greatness of soul'—and *katnuth demohin*—'diminution of soul'—and some would consider the fluctuating nature of faith to be essential to any deeply felt religious response.[1] But, as the Hasidim go on to teach, the profundity of his 'greatness of soul' experience gives man the strength to emerge from the mire of despair in his 'diminution of soul' state). Sir Arthur Eddington has finely said: 'Theological or anti-theological argument to prove or disprove the existence of a deity seems to me to occupy itself largely with skating among the difficulties caused by our making a fetish of this word. It is all so irrelevant to the assurance for which we hunger. In the case of our human friends we take their existence for granted, not caring whether it is proven or not. Our

[1] See the profound remarks of Dr. A. Altmann in his paper: *The Modern Analysis of Faith* delivered to the 9th Conference of Anglo-Jewish Preachers, 1951.

relationship is such that we could read philosophical arguments designed to prove the non-existence of each other, and perhaps even be convinced by them—and then laugh together over so odd a conclusion. I think that it is something of the same sort of security we should seek in our relationship with God. The most flawless proof for the existence of God is not substitute for it; and if we have that relationship, the most convincing disproof is turned harmlessly aside. If I may say it with reverence, the soul and God laugh together over so odd a conclusion.'[1]

But the concept 'my God' requires the support of 'God of my fathers'. Religion is impoverished and deprived of much of its grandeur unless the life of the individual worshipper is linked with the generations of those who worshipped long before he came on to the scene. The late Stephen Wise, in his autobiography, describes his emotions when reading the Shema. The Jew when reciting: 'Hear O Israel, the Lord our God, the Lord is One', Wise reminds us, is not simply voicing a bare theological formula. By repeating the identical words used by Jews since the earliest times he relives the experience of his forbears. He is at one with the Jews who uttered those words in Synagogues all over the world; he is at one with the martyrs and heroes of Israel who gave their lives rather than be false to those words; he is at one with the Jew who dies with these words on his lips as well as with the little Jewish child who is taught to repeat them for the first time. 'My God' becomes 'the God of the fathers'. Both concepts are essential to Jewish piety the one giving strength to the other. 'Even an individual man of Israel who has learned words of Torah, but has gone to other places (and has neglected the Torah) let him not be ashamed of coming back, for he may well say: "To the inheritance of my fathers I return". They made a similitude concerning this: Whereunto is this like? To a prince who had gone to a province of the sea: even after a hundred years he is not ashamed to return, for thus he says: 'To the inheritance of my fathers I return".'[2]

[1] *Science and the Unseen World*, Lond., 1929, p. 49f.
[2] Sifre, Deut., 33. 4.

CHAPTER IV

Is Religious Faith an Illusion?

Most people today are aware of the attack on religion by some psychologists, Freud in particular. In his *Totem and Taboo* (1913), *The Future of an Illusion* (1928) and *Moses and Monotheism* (1939), Freud develops his unflattering thesis that religion is an illusion, a lingering, childish desire for a 'Father substitute', the fruit of repressed desires and infantile impulses, and that the day must come when men will rid themselves of this unreal prop and, casting out fear, learn to stand on their own feet. Freudian ideas have by now penetrated to the market-place so that one encounters increasingly the suggestion that religious belief is nothing more than wishful thinking, that we believe because we want to, not because there is good ground for belief, that we are no better than the fox-hunter who believes that hunting is good for the fox or the cigar addict who believes that the ash he drops is good for the carpet.

The Freudian attack is countered by religious thinkers who note that Freud was convinced that religious belief is illusory on other than psycho-analytic grounds. The question Freud sets out to answer in his work on religion is: since God does not exist why do men believe in Him? But the believer rejects Freud's basic premise as a wholly gratuitous assumption. For him religion rests on far surer grounds than the desire to believe. He is convinced, as we have seen, that there are at least as good reasons for belief as for unbelief.

Perhaps the best popular statement of the religious reply to Freud is given by Leslie D. Weatherhead.[1] Weatherhead writes, of course, from the standpoint of his own faith—indeed he claims that Freud's views on religion are the result of a revolt against the Orthodox Jewish background he knew as a

[1] *Psychology, Religion and Healing*, p. 400f.

child[1]—but in fact, Weatherhead's valuable threefold answer is applicable in even greater measure to Judaism. With due acknowledgements to Weatherhead, we can say:

(1) *To desire a father does not invalidate the fact that he may exist*, any more than to desire food is proof that food does not exist. In fact, as we have noted in the previous chapter, the very hunger for God is an indication of His existence. If we are to reject as false every opinion which gives pleasure or satisfaction to those who hold it we should be compelled to reject much else besides religious ideas.

(2) *Judaism is a historical religion, not a religion created to fill a need*. It is more than a little difficult to understand how Judaism came about, how the teachings of the Torah and the Prophets, so different from contemporary views of religion, came to be expressed in the way they were without God's Self-disclosure, without Revelation. Among others, Ezekiel Kaufmann has convincingly demonstrated, in his *Toledoth Ha-'Emunah Ha-Yisraelith* the uniqueness of Israel's conception. A whole people from the beginnings of its history recognises God and brings paganism to an end. Israel's monotheism has no roots in the pagan world, the dominant trend of Protestant Bible Studies notwithstanding. The irrefutable arguments in support of this are there to be studied in Kaufmann's massive work. Add to this the astonishing persistence of Judaism and the stubborn survival of the Jews in the teeth of adversity and there is much truth in the saying attributed to Napoleon's page that the strongest argument for the existence of God is the existence of the Jews!

(3) *Judaism is too austere in its demands to be the kind of illusion men invent*. If one thinks of the martyrdom of Jewry throughout the ages, of the self-denial practised by millions of Jews and Jewesses in submission to the difficult Torah discipline, of the students who spent laborious days and nights in the study of the Talmud, of the Jews in western lands who sacrificed the most lucrative careers and promising ambitions

[1] But Freud's niece, in an autobiographical sketch, denies that Freud's parents were orthodox or that their household was pious (see *Commentary*, May, 1956, pp. 418f). H. L. Philp in his valuable *Freud and Religious Belief*, Lond., 1956, adopts the attitude that Freud's bias in favour of atheism was the product of his "free-thinking" home background.

rather than be faithless to their religion, it is hard to see why, if an illusion had to be invented, it should be such a rigorous one. Many of the prayers begin with the words 'Our Father, our King'—God is not alone the kindly, protective Father, He is also the King Who makes demands on His subjects. The Rabbis knew of the distinction between the religion which offers security and which is a call to adventure, a journey into the unknown, the staking of one's life, when they taught that Abraham, unlike Noah who required 'a support' and who 'walked *with* God', walked '*before* God'. In fact, many have argued that far from religious belief being an illusion, unbelief is an attempt to avoid the difficult demands of the Torah by denying the premises on which they are based. For many people the idea that there is no God, that, in the words of the Rabbis, there is no 'judge and judgment', is a more comfortable system than one in which man is responsible for what he makes of his life. In this connection the verse has been quoted: 'Let the wicked forsake his way, and the unrighteous man his thoughts',[1] i.e. the *thoughts* of the unrighteous, his denial of God, is the fruit of his choice of an evil *way*. If he will only forsake his *way* he will automatically abandon his sceptical *thoughts*. In the same spirit the saintly *Haphetz Hayyim* removed the whole question of unbelief from the intellectual to the moral plane when he said that for the man of faith there are no problems while for the man who lacks faith there are no solutions. It seems to me that this is to go too far in the opposite direction. After all there are honest doubters, men who would desire nothing more than to have faith, and Maimonides did write his guide for such people, but the point is well taken that there are as good reasons for suggesting that atheism is an illusion as for suggesting that religious faith is an illusion.[2]

[1] Is. lv. 7.

[2] The other great school of modern psychology, founded by C. G. Jung is far more sympathetic to the religious outlook. Jung's standpoint is, of course, empirical. He is not concerned with theology. But there is much in his theory of the Unconscious that is supplementary to a religious outlook. I am not competent, nor is this work the place, to discuss this in detail. The interested reader is referred to the erudite work *God and the Unconscious*, Lond., 1953, by Victor White, who writes from the Catholic angle and whose work has received the ecclesiastical *imprimatur* but which will be found stimulating and suggestive by Jews if Jewish symbols are substituted for Christian ones.

So far we have dealt with the relation between modern psychological theories and faith itself. It is appropriate here to note a number of studies by Freudians on some of the specifically Jewish rituals. In these studies psycho-analytic theories are used to explain the deeper motives which, it is alleged, animate the observant Jew. One of the pioneers in this field was Theodor Reik, a disciple of Freud, whose papers on this subject have been collected and translated into English in two volumes.[1] Reik's theories, together with those of other psychoanalysts, have been carefully summarised and criticised in an essay by Abraham Cronbach.[2] In this essay, Cronbach gives a full bibliography of the most important psycho-analytic investigations of Jewish interest. As an example of Reik's method and its inadequacies, his interpretation of Kol Nidre may be quoted.

One of the most intriguing questions connected with Kol Nidre is how it came about that a bare, almost juridical formula, should have been accompanied by a deeply affecting melody. The answer usually given is to deny any real association between the formula and its melody, the plaintive tones of the latter having reference not to the annulment of vows, but to the ushering in of the awe-inspiring Day of Atonement. But this leaves unsolved the problem of why the services of the day should begin with a formula having no relevance to them. As has often been noted, the Talmudic reference to a declaration of annulment of vows speaks of 'the beginning of the year', not of Yom Kippur. 'Whoever wishes all the vows he may make throughout the year to be null and void shall come at the beginning of the year and say: "May all the vows which I shall vow be annulled".'[3]

Reik's solution to the problem, in an essay which combines a fairly comprehensive historical account of Kol Nidre with a psycho-analytic interpretation of the rite, can briefly be summarised as follows: Zechariah Frankel, in his famous *Die Eidesleistung der Juden*, argues that the Kol Nidre formula is

---

[1] *Ritual*, Lond., 1931, and *Dogma and Compulsion*, N.Y., 1951.
[2] *Psychoanalytic Study of Judaism*, in Hebrew Union College Annual, Vol. VIII–IX, 1931–2.
[3] Ned. 23b.

for the purpose of fighting against, or, more correctly, of freeing oneself from hasty and impossible vows. In the light of Freudian theory this is interpreted to mean that the Kol Nidre is the expression of a sub-conscious desire on the part of the congregation to violate its vows.

It is possible that in the same person impulses emerge which suddenly call into question all moral gain and all carefully defended acquirements. The term *ambivalence*, used by psycho-analysts, designates the circumstance that a person may like, and at the same time dislike, one and the same person or action. Thus at the beginning of the awesome day when Israel renews its covenant with God, people experience a resurging of vicious tendencies, a powerful impulse to cast off the yoke of Judaism precisely because the tension is great and the repression strong. Reik tellingly quotes the story of two Jews, who, having become bitter enemies owing to business differences, broke off all intercourse with each other. They met on Yom Kippur and, in obedience to the religious precept that enemies have to be reconciled to one another, one said to the other: 'Well, I wish you everything that you wish me'. 'Beginning again already?' was the retort. (This whole theory is connected by Reik with the Freudian idea of the *Urmord* and the primordial vow taken by the sons who, having slain the father, resolve never to repeat the deed. Critics of this notion have called attention to the total absence of any evidence upon which it could be based).[1]

Reik then considers the Kol Nidre to have been originally a *confession*, prefaced by some such prayer as 'See, we confess to Thee we are a congregation of perjurers!' or 'Lord hear us, we confess to Thee that we feel within us the wish not keep oaths and vows, etc. . . .' Summing up, Reik says: 'The acknowledgement of the wicked wish is really an appeal to God: it serves to support the prayer for pardon and mercy. God is to see how much His people are enmeshed in sin. The frailty of human nature, its relapse into sin, and the impossibility of completely renouncing the gratification of impulses is demonstrated to Him *ad oculos;* let Him take into considera-

[1] See especially H. L. Philp, *op. cit.*, pp. 38f.

tion these weaknesses, and thereby be more disposed to grant pardon and impunity'.

The first reaction of the layman is to reject this interpretation as far-fetched, as brilliant but tortuous. If Reik is right it is difficult to account for the fact that no version of the introductory prayer, which alone gives Kol Nidre its meaning, has come down to us. Yet if we cannot accept Reik's theory as to the *origin* of Kol Nidre it would be stupid to deny that subconscious impulses of the kind he mentions may have been *associated* with the formula and may account, in part at least, for the poignancy of the accompanying melody. There is a natural reaction to the revelation of hitherto unrecognised depths of perversity within us. It is said that when the Rosh Yeshiba of Mir heard the Freudian theories for the first time he remarked: 'Freud is quite brilliant but it seems to me that he seizes the soul by its underpants!' Yet to refuse off-hand to avail ourselves of such theories in an effort to understand Jewish practices is to close the door to the possibility of a more profound appreciation of the interaction of our faith on the deeper levels of human experience.

Another example of Reik's method is his long essay (in his *Dogma and Compulsion*) in which he tries to explain the significance of *Tefillin* and *Tzitzith*. Reik first gives a lucid account of what *Tefillin* and *Tzitzith* are, but his tone is that of one who has prejudged their 'primitive' character. Thus, at the beginning of the essay he writes: 'To us these objects appear no less peculiar than the praying gloves, prayer mills, and prayer pennants of the peoples of the Far East'. There are, in addition, a number of inaccuracies from which it seems that in spite of copious quotations from Talmudic and Rabbinic literature, Reik's knowledge is second-hand. He speaks of *Rabbi* Tam and *Rabbi* Raschi; he appears to think that the pious Jews who wear the two pairs of Tefillin have two *head* Tefillin only when, in fact, they have two *hand* Tefillin as well; the name *arba kamphot* [sic] is said to be that of the prayer shawl; he does not seem to know that Jews gave up wearing *Tzitzith* attached to their ordinary garments because such garments in Western lands were not 'four cornered'; the benediction over the *Tallith* is given as: 'who hast hallowed us by thy commandments and hast bidden us to wear garments with the *tzitzith* thereon' [sic]; and there are incorrect references to the sources.[1]

But we proceed to Reik's theory. He says that he was started on the right trail by an old book in German which gives a description of Jewish ceremonies and in which it is stated that the hairs of cows or calves are wound around the parchments of the Tefillin and one hair is allowed to stand out. On inquiring of a Rabbi of the purpose of this, the author of the book was informed that it had to do with the red heifer or with the calf which the Israelites worshipped in the wilderness. From this 'hint' Reik proceeds to identify the *Tefillin* and the *Tallith* with an ancient article of clothing or disguise which represented the wearer, symbolically, as a bull or an ox. The head *Tefillah* is said to be a relic, a survival, of a disguise which the Israelites adopted on certain occasions. The hand *Tefillah* would then represent the hoof of the ox; the leathern thong its hide; the woollen *Tallith* the substitute for the fleece of a ram, and the *Tzitzith* would be allusions to the animal's four legs, and the knotting of the threads would represent the joints [sic]. The *Tefillin* and *Tallith* were thus originally, in Reik's view, a substitute for the 'totemic pelt' which the ancient Israelites wore in order to identify themselves with their totemic god. When later on the worship of God suppressed the old totemistic ideas these latter were not eliminated but were 'amalgamated' and made use of in the new faith.

The very natural response of the observant Jew to 'rend his garments' on hearing this explanation should be resisted, for even were it proved conclusively that Reik's theory is true there is nothing basically shocking or offensive to the religious mind in the thought that the Torah uses for its own ends practices too deeply rooted in the life of the people to be utterly eradicated. A possible example of this is the law concerning the corners of the field.[2] The ancient farmer left a

---

[1] E.g. on page 183 the reference Yad. III, 15 is given whereas there are no more than 5 *mishnayoth* in Chapter III; on page 191 the reference is given as Ber. III, 5 but this has nothing whatsoever to do with *Tefillin*.

[2] Lev. xix. 9–10.

part of his field unharvested for the benefit of the demons, who, if allowed to go hungry, would be jealous of his good fortune. Instead of condemning this practice outright, the Torah urges the farmer to leave the corners of his field, not to the demons, but to the poor and the stranger.[1] It is well known that Maimonides was the great pioneer in the field of comparative religion by remarking on the way in which many of the observances of the Torah can be more clearly understood if viewed against the background of their time and seen as the divine agency for weaning mankind from the baser forms of religion to the worship of the true God. There is little to which the most orthodox Jew could take exception in the following words of Leo Baeck: 'Primitive and rudimentary forms have their value for the understanding of the *origin*, for the embryological history of religion. But for the purpose of *judging* and for the actual knowledge of the essence of an historical phenomenon, only the characteristic and classic forms may be considered. Only by following the course of its development can one determine what a religion comprises and what are its vital chords. The very thing, which, in the origin, constituted an exception, may frequently emerge in the course of history as the essential, as the most important, element. The characteristic peculiarity is only brought out with the passing of the centuries. It is a truism that "the child is father to the man", but not until we study its progress into manhood are we able to know what were the distinctive peculiarities of the child. The real significance of the Jewish religion lies in its ascent, in the height which it has reached and maintained, and not in the rudimentary forms out of which it has risen'.[2] So that even if Reik were correct the fact that in the Torah the *Tefillin* and *Tzitzith* stress among other things the sublime doctrine of the Imitation of God (for there is, of course, no actual reference to the alleged primitive idea of idolatrous identification) is but an added reason for the devout Jew to wear them daily.

But the fact is that Reik's preposterous theory cannot pro-

---

[1] Cf. Frazer's *The Golden Bough*, Vol. VII, pp. 234–5 and I. Heinemann's *Ta'ame Hamitzvoth*, Jer. 1949, p. 14.

[2] *The Essence of Judaism*, p. 13.

duce the slightest bit of evidence in its support (it is quoted here at length as an excellent illustration of the need for distinguishing between the very real achievements of the Freudians in opening new windows on the human mind and their pseudo-anthropological theories which cannot be dignified by the name of science). All the evidence quoted is from late Kabbalistic usage and this is carefully selected. (Reik himself states that this theory was suggested to him by the book in which reference is made to the protruding hair, it was, he says with heavy-handed humour, 'dragged in by the hair'). He overlooks, for instance, that in both the Bible and the Talmud there is the closest association of *Tefillin* and *Tzitzith* with *Mezuzah*. He speaks of the two head *Tefillin* of *Rashi* and *Rabenu Tam* as a trace of the two horns of the 'totemic animal' conveniently overlooking that there are two *hand Tefillin* as well. He speaks of the three and four *teeth* of the letter *Shin* on the head *Tefillah* as if this supported his theory. But in the Jewish sources these are called *yods*, never *teeth*. Reik himself mentions that silken *Tallethim* can be used. The preference for wool is because according to the Rabbis, 'garments' in the Bible are generally woollen garments. The whole theory is an elaborate piece of guesswork with no claim to scientific objectivity or careful weighing of evidence. However, as has been said, the extremely far-fetched nature of some of their hypotheses should not blind us to the value of some of the ideas of the Freudians for a deeper understanding of Judaism.

The theory of the conflict in man between the super-ego (the conscience) and the id (desire), for example, appears to be quite compatible with the Jewish view of human nature. Weatherhead, in his afore-mentioned book, compares man to one who inhabits a room, on the ceiling of which the super-ego in the attic knocks, demanding him to come up, and on the floor of which the id in the cellar knocks, demanding him to come down and respond to its needs, so that he is distracted and torn asunder. The way to mental health is to recognise both elements, and then make terms with them. A man must not yield to either completely, for neither would let the other have it all his own way. That which he *ought* to do and that which he *wants* to do must be co-ordinated in an 'ego-ideal', and then harmony can be restored. It is fruitful to compare this with rabbinic views on the conflict between the good and evil inclinations, between the *yetzer tob* and the *yetzer hara*, and the frank recognition of the latter's claim if used legitimately.[1]

To my knowledge no writers on this subject in English refer to the pioneer work of Alter Druyanov (1870–1938), who was probably the first Jewish scholar to discuss certain aspects of Jewish life in the light of psycho-analytic theory. Druyanov, in his two Hebrew essays on the subject,[2] gives a number of interesting examples of how complete submission to the demands of the super-ego can produce that exaggerated and pathological guilt which is so marked a feature of many neuroses. A scribe would repeatedly open the *Tefillin* he had sewn together because of the fear that he may have placed the *parashiyoth* in the wrong order. The same man would repeat every verse of the Shema many times out of fear that a mistake had been made in pronunciation. A rabbi refused to answer ritual questions because if he decided, for instance, that a hen brought before him was *kasher*, he was haunted by the fear that it may have been *terefah*, if *terefah* that it may have been *kasher*.

The learned Rabbi Joshua Leib Diskin (1818–1898) 'analysed' a pious Jewish woman, who tasted tallow in whatever she ate. It transpired that as a young girl she had been a servant in the household of a wealthy man. Once, when milking the cow by candlelight, the candle fell into the pail of milk, and, fearing the wrath of her mistress, she allowed the members of the family to drink the milk. The rabbi assured her that she had committed no wrong, for the small amount of tallow had become neutralised in the milk (*batel beshishim*), her peace of mind was restored and the symptoms disappeared. Finally, Druyanov considers 'Purim Torah', the frivolous manipulation of Biblical texts and Rabbinic sayings on the

---

[1] For a useful selection in English of the relevant material see Schechter's *Some Aspects of Rabbinic Theology*, Chapters XV and XVI, and Montefiore and Loewe's *A Rabbinic Anthology*, Chapter XI.

[2] *Reshumoth*, Vol. I, Odessa, 1918, pp. 199-204, Vol. II, Tel Aviv, pp. 303–357.

festival of Purim, to be an attempt by scholars to obtain relief from the oppressive demands of the super-ego.

The Torah was not given to the ministering angels, say the Rabbis. Judaism controls life but does not deny it. Every part of human nature can find fulfilment within its range. The recognition of the tension existing in the human soul, far from being detrimental to the religious life, is an essential ingredient in it. As Reik, in his essay on Kol Nidre, concludes, the covenant, the *Brith* between God and Israel is renewed on Yom Kippur, which begins with the gloomy sounds of the Kol Nidre, telling of oppressive guilt, but expressing submission and repentance, in order to end in the loud announcement of the uniqueness of God.

CHAPTER V

The Problem of Pain

THE severest obstacle to faith in God is undoubtedly the problem of suffering and pain. As St. Augustine puts it: Either God can prevent suffering and does not do so, in which case He cannot be good. Or he wishes to prevent suffering and cannot do so, in which case He cannot be omnipotent! The Rabbis before Augustine discuss the problem of why the righteous suffer and the wicked prosper, the Biblical books deal with the same question, and it would be true to say that thinking men have been puzzled by the mysterious way in which God moves ever since men began to believe in the existence of a Beneficent Creator. To see doctors pitting their skill against foul diseases, statesmen struggling to prevent war, social reformers fighting to clear the slums and combat misery and squalor, and rescue workers trying to bring succour to the trapped and maimed after a railway accident, is to be confronted with the burning question: 'Shall mortal man be more just than God? shall a man be more pure than his maker?'[1] If human beings fight evil how can a Benevolent God allow evil to exist in the first place?

It would be intolerably glib to attempt to give smooth answers to this terrible question. Were it not for the problem of pain the surface of serene faith would scarcely be ruffled. It is chiefly because of this problem that men doubt. The religious apologist dare not embark on a discussion of this problem without constantly being aware that he is probing an open wound, arguing about the blood and tears of living men and women, face to face with the greatest mystery. It is so fatally easy for a writer on this theme to fall into the trap of arrogantly intimating that he is an initiate who knows secrets denied to others. It is, therefore, with the greatest trepidation that the following observations are offered—they cannot be

[1] Job. iv. 17.

44

called more than casual observations and these too not the author's original thoughts but a restatement of what great and good men have had to say on the question.

First, we have to note three arguments which have been frequently advanced as a complete, or partial solution of the problem of pain but which will not bear too close an examination.

(1) *That pain is a punishment for sin.*

The most common attempt to explain suffering is to look upon it as evidence of divine displeasure, as God's way of chastising a man for his sins. Suffering as a punishment for sin is met with in the Bible—Miriam becomes leprous because she slandered Moses; David loses the child he had from Bath Sheba; Ahab is slain in battle because he stole the vineyard from Naboth; the prophets foretell the doom that will befall sinful nations—'Thus saith the Lord: For three transgressions of . . . Yea, for four, I will not reverse it. . . .'[1] In the Rabbinic literature, there are numerous references to the doctrine of 'measure for measure', that God visits people with pain and suffering because they have sinned.

This doctrine need not be interpreted in any vindictive sense; the purpose of the punishment, it is frequently stated, is that the sinner repent. (When we violently shake a man who has fallen into a dead faint, is it our intention to chastise him or to revive him? as the famous eighteenth century preacher, Jonathan Eibeschütz, put it). 'But if the wicked turn from all sins that he hath committed, and keep all my statutes, and do that which is lawful and right, he shall surely live, he shall not die. None of his transgressions that he hath committed shall be remembered against him; for his righteousness that he hath done he shall live. Have I any pleasure at all that the wicked should die? saith the Lord God; and not rather that he should return from his ways and live?'[2] And it has often received the interpretation that sin carries with it the seeds of dissolution; that God has so created the world that a failure to obey His laws in the moral sphere has the same kind of effect as the

---

[1] Amos i. 3f.
[2] Ez. xviii. 21–23.

failure to obey them in the natural sphere. If a man drinks
poison his death is not a *punishment* for drinking.

But while the doctrine of reward and punishment is a cardinal principle of the Jewish faith, the obvious objection to it
being used as an *explanation* of the existence of pain is the
hard fact that it is so often the good who suffer and the wicked
who appear to escape. The whole of the book of Job has as
one of its aims the refutation of the view that a man's suffering can always be attributed to his sins. Job is a good man
whose friends try to explain his severe sufferings, the loss of
his children and his worldly goods and the racking of his body
by pain, as punishment for his sins.

> Then answered Eliphaz the Temanite, and said:
> If one venture a word unto thee, wilt thou be weary?
> But who can withhold himself from speaking?
> Behold, thou hast instructed many,
> And thou hast strengthened the weak hands.
> Thy words have upholden him that was falling,
> And thou hast strengthened the feeble knees.
> But now it is come unto thee, and thou art weary;
> It toucheth thee, and thou art affrighted.
> Is not thy fear of God thy confidence,
> And thy hope the integrity of thy ways?
> Remember, I pray thee, who ever perished, being innocent?
> Or where were the upright cut off?[1]

But Job cannot accept these suggestions that he suffers because he is a sinner; his whole being cries out against a punishment that in no way fits the crime. He cannot believe that the
greater the suffering the greater the sin, for his reason tells
him that if he is no better than his fellows he is certainly not
so much worse. The Rabbis of the Talmud teach that to act
as Job's comforters did is to commit the offence of 'wrong-
ing with words'.[2] The second century teacher, R. Yannai,
gave expression to the common sense rejection of the all too
simple explanation of 'tit for tat' when he said: 'It is not in
our power to explain either the prosperity of the wicked or
the afflictions of the righteous'.[3]

---

[1] Job. iv. 1–7.   [2] B.M. 58b.   [3] Aboth IV. 19.

(2) *That pain is not evil because it serves as a warning.*

A train crashes and many lives are lost, a 'plane engine fails and its passengers hurtle to their death, with the result that inquiries are held to discover the causes of these tragedies and train and plane journeys are made safer in the future. An aching tooth gives its possessor no rest until he visits the dentist, who, acting in time, saves the tooth. These are examples of pain serving as a warning so that evil becomes the handmaid of good. But, granted the beneficial effects of some kinds of pain, it simply will not do to quote examples such as these as a solution to the whole problem of pain. For one thing such an argument would ignore those many tragic cases where pain occurs too late to serve as a warning—the lives of some victims of cancer would have been saved were it not for the fact that the dread disease gives no indication of its presence in the early stages when its progress can be halted. Furthermore, the idea that pain is nature's warning gives us no answer to the question of why the greater pain should be allowed to exist that its action be forestalled by the lesser.

(3) *That there is no extension of pain.*

It has sometimes been suggested that the problem of pain is not so acute because there is no extension of pain. Pain, it is argued, can only be felt because mind exists—a corpse does not and cannot feel pain. But if suffering is dependent on mind then it follows that when two people suffer, the only pain experienced is the pain in the mind of each. There is no more pain in existence, as it were, when two suffer than when one suffers. If a thousand people starve to death there is no such thing as a conglomeration of a thousand pains for the pain occurs in the mind of each individual and it cannot be added together. There is no greater total of pain than that felt by the individual who suffers the most. C. S. Lewis, in his provocative book on this subject, puts it as follows: 'We must never make the problem of pain worse than it is by vague talk about the "unimaginable sum of human misery". Suppose that I have a toothache of intensity x: and suppose that you, who are seated beside me, also begin to have a toothache of intensity x. You may, if you choose, say that the total amount of pain in the room is now $2x$. But you must remember that no one is suffering $2x$: search all time and all space and you will not find that composite pain in anyone's consciousness. There is no such thing as a sum of suffering, for no one suffers it. When we have reached the maximum that a single person can suffer, we have, no doubt, reached something very horrible, but we have reached all the suffering there ever can be in the universe. The addition of a million fellow-sufferers adds no more pain'.[1] But valid though this argument is in reducing the scale of the problem the difficulty remains of how a benevolent God can tolerate the pain and anguish of even one human being—quite apart from the obvious objection that a human being who condemns many people to suffering is generally considered to be a worse person than he who is responsible for the sufferings of a few. A Genghis Khan or a Hitler meets, with justice, a far greater degree of execration than the man who murders his next door neighbour.

The three 'explanations' just referred to do little to help us. We turn now to some of the more important observations that have been made by religious thinkers in their quest for a theodicy. First, a distinction must be made between two kinds of pain and evil—that caused by man and that independent of man. When the problem of pain is discussed among Jews today the example frequently quoted is that of the six million Jews murdered by the Nazis. How can God have allowed such things to happen? But terrible though this problem is, it is, in one sense, easier to understand than that of pain caused by 'nature'. For we can obtain some glimmer of understanding concerning why God allows man to do evil, for only by being free to choose evil can he be free to choose good. If, for

---

[1] *The Problem of Pain*, Lond., 1940, pp. 103–4. This idea appears to have been anticipated in a talmudic discussion. The ruling is given that in the case of false witnesses, who are to be punished by receiving the imposition they desired to be inflicted on their victim (Deut. xix. 19), monetary impositions are shared among the offenders, but the lashes of a flogging are not shared among the offenders. If, for instance, three men gave false witness against a person that he owed 300 *zuz* they divide the corresponding damages proportionately among them—they would pay 100 *zuz* each. But if they gave evidence that he was liable to a flogging of thirty-nine lashes, each one would receive not thirteen but thirty-nine lashes. The difference between the cases is stated as follows: '*Money can be united into one total, whereas lashes cannot be united into one total*' (Makk. 5a).

example, every time a man tried to stab his fellow the knife became blunt; every time he fired a revolver to harm another the weapon misfired; every time he put his hand into his neighbour's pocket to steal he could not withdraw it; every time he endeavoured to be cruel to others his designs were miraculously frustrated; then the sheer impossibility of committing evil actions would inevitably propel men in the direction of the good and there would be little or no merit in doing good. The result of God forcibly restraining men from doing evil would be, it is true, the effective banishment of such evil but it would also mean the just as effective banishment of the good which men do. Conceivably God could have created men without freedom of choice but, in the religious view, it is this freedom that is man's pride and glory, without which he cannot be God-like. God, evidently, does not wish to be served by automata but by freely responding creatures who can reach out for His goodness by the free action of their wills. 'Everything', said R. Haninah, 'is in the power of Heaven save the fear of Heaven'.[1] R. Simeon ben Lakish taught that he who wishes to lead an unclean life has the door open to him; but he who wishes to lead a pure life is helped Divinely.[2] It is an awful but convincing thought that without the power to produce its sinners mankind could not produce its saints; without the risk of a Hitler there could not have been a Ghandi; and, if it be argued that the price is far too high, the religious answer would be that for man to be God-like and share in His goodness for ever, no price is too high. A talking human, said the Maggid of Meseritz, occasions no surprise, a talking bird evokes astonishment and admiration. So too a virtuous angel is no novelty in the realm of the spirit but God and all His angels rejoice at the virtuous man who lives the good life despite his propensity for evil.

So much for the evil caused by man. But what of evil caused by 'act of God'? By floods ruthlessly sweeping away that which has been laboriously built up; by earthquakes destroying man and his possessions; what of the diseases and the anguish, not of his making, by which the face of man is

[1] Ber. 33b.
[2] Sabb. 104a.

blackened? It is not suggested by any thinking religious person that a complete and satisfactory solution to this can ever be found. There is much in the idea that such difficulties are inherent in the religious outlook for how can the finite mind of man comprehend the Infinite? A faith without 'difficulty' —one perfectly clear to humans—would certainly be false for its scope would be purely human with no room for man's encounter with the divine. 'If I knew Him I would be Him' wrote a mediaeval Jewish thinker. But though a complete solution must, in the nature of the case, elude us, the following considerations, advanced by religious thinkers, have been found helpful to many.

(1) *That suffering ennobles.*

'Happy is the man whom Thou chastenest, O Lord, and teachest him out of Thy Law'.[1] The Psalmist means not alone that God afflicts man in order to recall him to his duty, but the deeper idea that the worth of man is most clearly observed when he conquers adversity and refuses to allow it to deter him from the service of God and his fellows. It is the idea contained in the ancient narrative of God 'testing' Abraham,[2] which has to be understood not in the sense of God desiring some information about Abraham's character He did not already possess, but as an opportunity for Abraham to demonstrate his faith in God. The Rabbis speak in this connection of a potter testing his wares; he taps the good quality ware with his hammer to test its durability without fearing the breakage that would certainly result if such treatment were given to inferior ware.[3] Or they vary the metaphor by comparing Abraham to a vial of precious perfume which cannot be allowed to rest on the shelf undisturbed but must be moved from place to place if men are to benefit from its fragrance.[4]

A man who had never suffered would have to be pitied rather than envied for he would have lived always on the superficial plane, not knowing life's bitterness he could never know its sweetness, his full potentialities would remain unrealised. It would be both unfair and unjust to the saint to see his rejoicing in suffering as the expression of a masochistic

1 Ps. xciv. 12.   3 B.R. 55.2.
2 Gen. xxii. 1–19.   4 B.R. 39. 2

urge or the need for making life's pleasures more piquant by the sauce of pain. The man who can sincerely exclaim 'Though He slay me, yet will I trust in Him'[1] is in the very act of self-denial and self-sacrifice fulfilling that higher self which delights in sheer disinterested giving. There is a divine spark in man which refuses to allow him to be completely satisfied unless he gives himself in the service of the highest.

The Talmudic Rabbis describe the kind of suffering that ennobles as 'chastenings of love'; though in speaking too of 'chastenings which are not of love' they were sufficiently realistic to recognise that suffering does not invariably ennoble and that the doctrine is no complete answer to the problem of pain. One Rabbi taught that chastenings of love are those which do not interrupt a man's study of the Torah, another Rabbi said those which do not interfere with his prayers.[2] The second century teacher, R. Simeon ben Yohai, said that the Holy One, blessed is He, gave Israel three precious gifts, and all of them were given only through sufferings—the Torah, the Land of Israel and the World to Come.[3] Yet, in the same Talmudic passage it is stated that when R. Hiyya bar Abba fell ill he was asked by his friend R. Johanan: 'Are your sufferings welcome to you?', 'Neither they nor their reward' was his reply. For suffering can sour a man's character as well as improve it!

The Hasidic teachers, in particular, dwell on this aspect of suffering. The founder of the Hasidic movement, the *Besht*, once said that the Hebrew word for 'light' is *Tzohar* and the word for 'anguish' *Tzarah*. The same three Hebrew letters are used in both these words. For, said the *Besht*, it is the function of the good Jew to turn his sufferings to good account, to change darkness into light, to convert *Tzarah* into *Tzohar*.

(2) *Without suffering there would be no sympathy.*

The finest human qualities can only be called into play as a result of suffering. The exercise of the charitable instincts, sympathy for the downtrodden, heroism in the face of danger, self-sacrifice in the pursuit of ideals, would all be impossible if evil were non-existent. Without social evils there could be no social workers, without poverty there could be no bene-

---

[1] Job. xiii. 15. [2] Ber. 5a. [3] Ber. *ibid.*

factors of the poor, without the guillotine there could be no
Sidney Carton, without the cruel Arctic night no Captain
Oates—as Hermann Cohen put it, without *Leid* there could
be no *Mitleid*. The *Besht* was once asked by his followers
why God permits men to doubt His existence. His answer was
that if men could never doubt God's providence then the
power of faith would be such that men would have it not
alone when they themselves were in trouble, when it is commendable, but when their fellows were in trouble, so that it
would preclude charity and benevolence.

This view is expressed in the following two Rabbinic
anecdotes. The Roman Governor of Palestine, Turnus Rufus,
asked R. Akiba: 'If thy God loves the poor why does He not
alleviate their suffering?' (No doubt there is a reference here
to the notion current in the Roman world, that the poor are
stricken with poverty because the gods are displeased with
them so that it would be blasphemous to help them, an attempt
to frustrate the will of the gods). Akiba's answer was, so that
those who help the poor may gain merit![1] It is a typical Jewish
doctrine that the poor man gives more than he receives. It is
further said that the same Turnus Rufus asked R. Akiba:
'Which are more to be admired the works of God or the
works of men?' To his surprise the Jewish sage replied: 'The
works of men'. And, in illustration, Akiba ordered to be
brought before them ears of corn and fine, freshly baked cakes.
'These,' he said, 'are the works of God, and these the works
of men. Which are to be more admired?' And he had brought
before them bundles of raw flax and finely spun linen garments and said: 'These are the works of God and these the
works of men. Which are to be more admired?'[2] This thought
runs right through the classical Jewish literature, that God
wants man to co-operate with Him, as it were, in the conquest
of pain, suffering and disease, and in this way to become, in
the expressive words of the Rabbis, 'a partner with God in
the work of Creation'.[3]

(3) *That suffering has its place in God's plan.*

It is an idea common to all the great faiths that there is a
plan and a purpose to life and that if only we could know

[1] B.B. 10a.   [2] Mid. Tanh. *Tazria'* 7, ed. Buber. Lev. p. 35.
[3] Sabb. 119b.

that plan we would understand that what appears to be meaningless is meaningful, that what appears to us as waste has its
purpose, and that when God's intention is fully realised evil is
transmuted into good. Whatever God does is for the best, is
said to have been the maxim of a Jewish saint. The Mishnah
rules that God is to be praised not alone when a man meets
with success. Even when he meets with adversity he must
bow his head in worship.[1]

The idea of a divine plan reminds us that our vision is
partial. We see only a tiny fragment of reality. If only we
could see the human scene as God sees it we would recognise
that every blow of fate against which we cried out in pain
was a brick in the splendid edifice of the good which God is
erecting through us. In one sense this is no more than a confession of defeat. It is simply a restatement of the view that we
cannot know the solution to the problem of pain. But in
another sense, while it contributes nothing towards a solution,
it helps us to understand that there *is* a solution, only we
cannot see it. The idea of a *plan* helps to reassure us
that we are not the playthings of chance. We gain in
strength to bear suffering if we know that it is not without
purpose.

In this connection there is a thought-provoking illustration
given by Edwyn Bevan. Bevan compares man's vision of God
to a dog's vision of his human master. 'In the dog's association
with his master there are some fields of activity which come
within the range of the dog's understanding, while there are
other fields in which the dog does not and cannot comprehend what his master is about. What the dog does come to
feel and know, even with his limited intelligence, if he is a
good dog and his master a good master, is that he is in the
service of a being immeasurably superior to the dog himself;
and from this intuition the dog—mere dog though he is—
draws an intellectual and moral conclusion. His intellectual
conclusion is that his master's unintelligible acts and orders
are likely to be as wise as those which the dog can understand have always proved to be. The dog's moral conclusion
is that it is its own duty to take this superior being's acts and

[1] Ber. ix. 5.

orders on trust—always obeying the orders with alacrity and
acquiescing in the acts with resignation.'[1]

The Jewish doctrine of the After-life will be considered in
a later chapter, but it must here be said that for this idea of a
divine plan to be at all meaningful it must involve the full
working out of that plan in the realm of *Eternity*. For it would
be hideously unfair to justify the sufferings of a good man
solely on the grounds that in the working out of God's plan
benefit results from them to other men here on earth. They
may, indeed, be of such benefit but our deepest feelings revolt
against the notion of a vicarious atonement in which the
victim receives compensation for his sufferings neither in this
world nor the next. (This is not to say, of course, that the
'compensation' he will receive in the next world is to be
understood in any mercenary sense).[2]

(4) *That suffering is the result of God's withdrawal.*

The Kabbalists grappled with the problem of evil. In the
Kabbalistic school founded by Isaac Luria (1534–1572) and
his disciple Hayyim Vital (1543–1620) the doctrine of
Tzimtzum—of God's *withdrawal* 'from Himself into Himself'
that the finite universe may emerge—was developed, and this
doctrine has a number of important ideas affecting our problem. Briefly stated, the doctrine of *Tzimtzum*[3] seeks to
explain how the Infinite could have produced a finite world.
How could an imperfect world of error and evil have emerged
from the Perfectly True and the Perfectly Good? If God is
everywhere, how can there be a world at all? The answer of
Tzimtzum is as follows.

God, the supremely Good and Benevolent 'requires' beings
other than Himself to be the recipients of His bounty, for it
belongs to the Essence of a supremely good Being to give of
that goodness to others. But for these 'others' to come into
being God has to withdraw, as it were, into Himself to make
room for the finite world and the finite creatures who inhabit
it, for nothing can exist in the full splendour of His infinite

[1] Quoted by Arnold J. Toynbee in *A Study of History*, Vol. X, O.U.P.,
1954, p. 1 n. 3.
[2] See below, p. 121.
[3] See Gershom G. Scholem: *Major Trends in Jewish Mysticism*, 3rd ed.,
Lond., 1955, pp. 260f.

light. In this view, Time and Space emerged in the primordial 'Space' left as the result of God's withdrawal. But just as nothing can endure in God's Presence, nothing can exist without the sustaining light of His presence. Hence it is suggested, a thin ray of divine light penetrates into the 'empty space' left by God's withdrawal, but this, while sufficiently strong to sustain the world, is not so powerful as to cause it to dissolve into nothingness.

All the evil in life is the result of God's withdrawal, for that is precisely what evil is, the absence of God, the All-Good. But the withdrawal itself is an act of divine mercy for without it there could not have existed creatures other than God whom He could benefit. This is the great paradox at the heart of the matter, that while the withdrawal of God's light is bound to produce evil, without that withdrawal there could have been no *good*, for there would have been no recipients of that good.

J. L. Mackie, in a profound discussion of the problem of pain,[1] sums up the problem as follows. 'In its simplest form the problem is this: God is Omnipotent; God is Wholly Good; and yet evil exists. Adequate solutions implicitly reject one of the constituent propositions'. No adequate Jewish solution can reject the second of these propositions—Judaism insists that God is Wholly Good. Attempts have been made in Jewish, as well as in general, thought to deny the reality of evil but this is not very helpful for even if evil is an illusion the illusion is real enough. J. M. E. McTaggart rightly said: 'A delusion or an error which hid from us the goodness of the universe would itself be evil. And so there would be real evil after all'. The four solutions we have noted above all imply, in fact, that the idea of God's omnipotence must not be taken to mean that there are no limitations whatsoever but that God has all the power there is. To expect God to create a universe in which certain goods, impossible without the existence of evil, would exist without evil is to expect God to do the impossible. Now God can do what seems impossible to us but He cannot do what is impossible to Him, not because He is limited but because the 'impossible to Him' cannot exist,

[1] *Evil and Omnipotence, Mind*, Vol. LXIV, No. 254, April, 1955, p. 200f.

the term is nonsense and cannot make sense simply because we attach the word God to the statement. Thus, even believers in God's omnipotence are obliged to say that this is voluntarily limited, to some extent, by His desire to give men freedom of choice and to create the kind of universe in which such choice can be exercised. Even God cannot create a universe in which man has the free choice between good and evil and in which, for all that, there is no evil, for this is a flagrant contradiction (see p. 111). But, of course, the difficulty remains. As we have seen it is *bound* to remain. As soon as we try to get to the heart of the problem we are halted by the evident absurdity of grasping the Unfathomable. But this does not mean that such 'solutions' are of no value. They can be compared to the flashings of lightning on a dark night which do make the road ahead a little more negotiable. In the words of one of the early Hasidim: 'God remains the Hidden God but when man knows that He is Hidden He is not truly Hidden'![1]

[1] Mention must be made of the problem of animal suffering—of 'nature red in tooth and claw'—a specially difficult one for, as C. S. Lewis says, so far as we know beasts are incapable either of sin or virtue: therefore they can neither deserve pain nor be improved by it. Lewis (*The Problem of Pain*, pp. 117–131) questions whether the lower animals experience pain, though they appear to do so, for a distinction must be made between *sentience* and *consciousness*. But, as he remarks, it is certainly difficult to suppose that the apes, the elephant, and the higher domestic animals, have not, in some degree a self or soul which connects experiences and gives rise to rudimentary individuality. The Rabbis frequently mention *tzaar baale hayyim* 'animal suffering' and they condemn those guilty of causing it, though animals may be slaughtered to provide food for humans. Lewis and other Christian writers in treating of this aspect of the problem refer darkly to the old doctrine of a cosmic fall. 'When I consider the panorama of life, with all its strange and sometimes horrifying expressions, when I consider, for example, the life-histories of parasites, I have an overwhelming impression that something has gone wrong with creation, and not only with the human race; there is something demonic about the inexhaustible flood of life as well as something divine. There is, I am persuaded, some profound reality behind the doctrine of the fall and its cosmic results but it is beyond my power to conjecture what that reality can be.' (W. R. Matthews in *Christian Belief Today*, Lond., 1952, p. 106). While for obvious reasons Jews do not share the Christian preoccupation with the Fall, the idea of a cosmic fall before man came on to the scene is not unknown in Jewish sources, which speak e.g. of the 'rebellion of the sea' and the 'rebellion of the trees', see Ginzberg's *Legends of the Jews*, Vol. V, notes 73, 74, 75, pp. 26–29. The mediaeval thinkers debated whether animals are rewarded in the hereafter. Saadiah Gaon ('Emunoth Ve-Deoth', end of Book III) believes that there is such reward but Maimonides (*Guide*, III, 17) ridicules this notion, see Henry Malter: *Saadiah Gaon*, Philadelphia, 1942, n. 482, pp. 210–211, and the *Universal Jewish Encyclopædia*, Vol. I, p. 330.

CHAPTER VI

The Torah and Modern Criticism

JUDAISM believes that God has revealed His will to mankind in the Torah. Not that it claims an exclusive possession of the knowledge of God's will by Israel—in the Bible God speaks to Adam and the other heroes who lived before the Sinaitic revelation just as He makes known His will to the heathen prophet, Balaam, after Sinai. The Midrash, indeed, records the saying of a Rabbi that Balaam was a greater prophet than Moses![1] The claim of traditional Judaism is that the Torah contains the fullest and most complete revelation of the divine will and that the Torah has not and never will be superseded by any other 'testament' or 'dispensation'.

What is meant by the Torah? On the whole, the word (from a root meaning 'to teach') is used in the classical Jewish sources in three distinct, but complementary, senses.

(1) The term is used of the Pentateuch—the first of the three divisions of the Hebrew Bible (the others being the Prophetical Books and the Hagiographa). Hence the common Hebrew term for the Bible is TANAKH, from the initial letters of Torah, Nebiim (the Prophets) and Kethubim (the Sacred Writings). The Rabbis speak of varying degrees of inspiration, the Pentateuch possessing the highest degree of sanctity, then the Prophets and then the Hagiographa. Thus Jewish practice prohibits the placing of a copy of any other Biblical book on top of a copy of the Pentateuch, similarly, it prohibits the placing of a book of the Hagiographa on top of a Prophetic book. In Synagogues everywhere, the place of honour is given to the Scroll of the Pentateuch, called the Sefer Torah—the Book of the Torah—which must be written by hand on specially prepared parchment in accordance with strict rules governing the script, the text and the manner of writing. It must also be noted that when the Rabbis spoke of the Torah in this sense, they meant not alone the written text

[1] Sifre to Deut., xxxiv. 10.

57

of the Pentateuch—the *Torah Shebikethab*—but its official interpretation, given in the first place to Moses on Sinai and handed down from generation to generation—the *Torah She -Be-'Al Peh*, the Oral Torah. The rules governing the ritual slaughter of animals, for example, though not mentioned explicitly in the Pentateuch, are considered to belong to the Torah and to have the status of Pentateuchal law because they were delivered orally to Moses. Similarly, those teachings derived by the process known as *Midrash* (from a root meaning 'to search', 'to inquire') in which the Torah text is closely examined so as to draw out its full implications, have the full status of Torah law.

(2) The term *Torah* is at times used for teachings found in the rest of the Bible, i.e. in the Prophetic books and the Hagiographa. And though there is evidence that these teachings were not accorded the full status of Torah law they possessed a higher degree of authority than rabbinic law. In the later rabbinic distinction, for example, between Torah and rabbinic laws (i.e. that in cases of doubt the stricter view is taken with regard to Torah law, the lenient view with regard to rabbinic law) the term 'Torah law' is made to embrace such duties as 'honouring the Sabbath', which is not found in the Pentateuch but in the book of Isaiah.[1]

(3) The word *Torah* is frequently used to embrace the sum-total of Jewish religious teaching, of everything that, in the words of the Rabbis, a diligent student adds to the understanding, elucidation, elaboration and application of Jewish religious truth. As Schechter says: 'In a certain manner it (the Torah) is extended even beyond the limits of the Scriptures. When certain Jewish Boswells apologised for observing the private life of their masters too closely, they said, "It is a Torah, which we are desirous of learning". In this sense it is used by another Rabbi, who maintained that even the everyday talk of the people in the Holy Land is a Torah (that is, it conveys an object lesson). For the poor man in Palestine, when applying to his neighbour for relief, was wont to say, "Acquire for thyself merit, or strengthen and purify thyself" (by helping me); thus implying the adage—that the man in want is just as

[1] Is. lviii. 13.

much performing an act of charity in receiving as his bene-
factor in giving. In the east of Europe we can, even today,
hear a member of the congregation, addressing his minister,
"Pray, tell me some Torah". The Rabbi would never answer
him by reciting verses from the Bible, but would feel it incum-
bent on him to give him some spiritual or allegorical explanation of a verse from the Scriptures, or would treat him to some
general remarks bearing upon morals and conduct."[1] Thus, the
Torah is conceived of as a great dynamic idea stimulating
Jewish minds and inspiring Jewish hearts to search for religious and moral truth and in finding that truth add to the
totality of Torah. The Torah is both creative in the lives of
Jews and in turn created by the Jews. It is a 'tree of life'
which, carefully tended by its devoted cultivators, nourished
by its fruit, produces new spiritual fruits in each generation.

While Judaism stands or falls on the belief in Revelation
there is no 'official' interpretation of the exact manner in which
God spoke to man. Dr. Hertz states the traditional position as
follows: 'Revelation means the unveiling of the character of
God to the children of men, accompanied by a binding
announcement of the Divine Will. All this is implied in the
Theistic position. If we think of the Universe as merely an
aggregate of blind forces, then there is, of course, no room
for communication of any kind between God and man. But
the moment we assert the existence of a Supreme Mind who is
the Fountain and Soul of all the infinite forms of matter and
life—Revelation, or communication between God and man,
becomes a logical and ethical necessity. The exact manner of
this super-natural communication between God and man, will
be conceived differently by different groups of believers.
Some will follow the Biblical accounts of Revelation in their
literal sense; others will accept the interpretation of these
Biblical accounts by Rabbis of Talmudic days, Jewish philosophers of the Middle Ages, or Jewish religious thinkers of
modern times. No interpretation, however, is valid or in con-
sonance with the Jewish Theistic position, which makes human
personality the *source* of such revelation'.[2]

---

[1] *Some Aspects of Rabbinic Theology*, Lond., 1909, p. 125–126.
[2] *Commentary to the Prayer Book*, Lond., 1947, p. 252.

However, it is only right to remark that the traditional view of revelation is more closely defined than this quotation from Hertz would suggest. It is no doubt true that there is no official view as to the *manner* of revelation but until comparatively modern times there has been complete unanimity on the *matter*, the *content* of revelation. The *how* of revelation may have been debated; the *what* of revelation was never doubted. The whole of the Pentateuch was given to Moses on Sinai, or, according to some Rabbis, at intervals during the sojourn in the wilderness;[1] the Prophetic books contain God's message through His prophets; and the Sacred Writings were compiled under the influence of divine inspiration. And it is precisely here that the challenge of Bible Criticism is acute. The confidence of many people in the Bible as the Word of God has been shaken by modern critical investigations so that no work of Jewish apologetics, however limited in scope, can afford to fight shy of the problem. Let us first state the traditional view in somewhat greater detail and then note how this view has been challenged and the suggestions that have been made for a synthesis between the old and new insights.

The source of the traditional Jewish outlook on the authorship of the Biblical books is the following Talmudic passage,[2] the exact date of which is not known but which is certainly not later than the end of the second century c.e.

'Who wrote the Scriptures?—Moses wrote his own book and the portion of Balaam and Job. Joshua wrote the book which bears his name and the Book of Judges and Ruth. David wrote the Book of Psalms, including in it the works of the elders, namely, Adam, Melchizedek, Abraham, Moses, Haman, Yeduthan, Asaph, and the three sons of Korah. Jeremiah wrote the book which bears his name, the Book of Kings, and Lamentations. Hezekiah and his colleagues wrote Isaiah, Proverbs, the Song of Songs and Ecclesiastes. The Men of the Great Assembly wrote Ezekiel, the Twelve Minor Prophets, Daniel and the Scroll of Esther, Ezra wrote the book that bears his name and the genealogies of the Book of Chronicles up to his own time.'

[1] Hag. 6a-b, Sot. 37b, Zeb. 115b.
[2] B.B. 14b–15a.

In the subsequent Talmudic discussion, some of these statements are questioned, e.g. that Moses wrote the book of Job or that Joshua wrote the whole of the book which bears his name, or that Moses wrote the last eight verses of the Pentateuch recording his death and burial, but generally speaking the above is an accurate account of the Talmudic view. From this and numerous similar passages it is clear beyond doubt that the doctrine of 'Torah from Heaven'—*Torah Min Ha-Shamayim*—meant not alone that the Pentateuch is divinely inspired like the other Biblical books, but that God dictated the whole of it (with the possible exception of the last eight verses) to Moses. The following passage speaks for itself:

> '*Because he hath despised the word of the Lord*—this refers to him who maintains that the Torah is not from Heaven. And even if he asserts that the whole Torah is from Heaven, excepting a particular verse, which was not written by God but by Moses himself, he is included in *because he hath despised the word of the Lord*. And even if he admits that the whole Torah is from Heaven, excepting a single point, a particular *ad majus* deduction or a certain *gezerah shawah*,[1]—he is still included in *because he hath despised the word of the Lord*.'[2]

Even the text of the Pentateuch, carefully established by the group of scholars known as the Masorites, was zealously preserved and protected from change in the Synagogue. While, as we shall see, it was considered less heretical to question the accuracy of the Masoretic text than to cast doubts on the Mosaic authorship of the Pentateuch, the orthodox position was generally that the text in use in the Synagogue was that given to Moses on Sinai. To this day the liturgy contains, as a prayer to be recited when the Torah is elevated in the Synagogue, the words: 'And this is the Torah which Moses set before the children of Israel, according to the commandment of the Lord by the hand of Moses'.[3] Similarly the Jewish

---

[1] One of the exegetical principles by virtue of which, because in two pentateuchal passages words occur which are similar, both laws are subject to the same regulations and applications.

[2] Sanh. 99a.

[3] Singer's Prayer Book, p. 69.

confession of faith includes the words: 'I believe with perfect faith that the whole Torah, now in our possession, is the same that was given to Moses our Teacher, peace be unto him.'[1]

There is undoubtedly a certain grandeur about the traditional view. It is exceedingly reassuring to know that we can rely for guidance in matters of religion and morals on a divine book complete in every respect, which we possess together with a divine guarantee that its text is free from error. But this view has been seriously assailed by critical and historical investigations, as most people are today aware.

What is known as the Lower Criticism of the Bible has as its aim the establishment of a correct Biblical text. While no serious scholar would deny the essential reliability of the Masoretic text, it has long been recognised that the ancient versions such as the Septuagint—the Greek translation produced in Alexandria over two thousand years ago—the *Peshitta*, the early Syriac translation, and the Samaritan Pentateuch, frequently differ in their readings from the established text. These various readings often bear the stamp of probability upon them, and remove or lessen the difficulties of the Hebrew text. Again, parallel passages in the Biblical books, especially parallel lists of names, differ in such a manner as to make it clear that the variations are due to textual corruption. Then again there are passages in which the text, as it stands, cannot be translated without violence to the laws of grammar or is irreconcilable with the context or with other passages.[2] Because of these facts, modern scholarship accepts textual emendation as a valid method of interpretation. To give one or two examples:

(1) 'And on the seventh day God finished His work which He had made; and He rested on the seventh day from all His work which He had made'.[3] The difficulty here is obvious. If God ceased His creative activity *before* the Sabbath how can it be said that He finished His work 'on the seventh day'? The Septuagint reading is, however, 'And on the *sixth* day God finished His work'.

[1] Singer's Prayer Book, p. 90.
[2] See S. R. Driver: *Notes on the Hebrew Text of the Books of Samuel*, O.U.P., 1890, pp. ixf.   [3] Gen. ii. 2.

(2) 'And Moses built an altar, and called the name of it Adonainissi (the Lord is my banner). And he said: The hand upon the throne of the Lord: the Lord will have war with Amalek from generation to generation'.[1] The text of the second verse presents a difficulty. What is meant by 'the hand upon the throne of the Lord'? Furthermore, the usual Hebrew word for 'throne' is *kisse*, not the shorter *kes*, used here and nowhere else. But if, as S. D. Luzzatto quotes someone as saying (though Luzzatto disagrees with him), the letter *nun* is substituted for the letter *kaph*, which it closely resembles, the reading will be *nes*, meaning a 'banner'—the same word, in fact, as that used in the previous verse—instead of *kes*. The meaning would then be that the altar was called 'The Lord is my banner' (*nissi*) because the hand of the Lord was on His banner (*nes*).

(3) 'And Moses went and spoke these words unto all Israel'.[2] These words occur after Moses' farewell speech to his people before his death. The difficulty is, where did he go? But the Septuagint reads, by a transposition of two letters, *wayekhal* for *wayelekh*. The former means 'and he *finished*', the latter 'and he *went*'. Thus, we have the excellent reading: 'And Moses finished speaking these words unto all Israel', a reading that has been corroborated by one of the recently discovered Dead Sea fragments.

These alternative readings are by no means conclusive, and, of course, not every textual emendation is of value. On the whole the Masoretic text is far superior to the other versions. But the validity of the *principle* of emendation cannot be gainsaid. And this need not be a cause for alarm. The Talmud itself gives a number of variant readings: the nineteenth century scholar, R. Akiba Eger, gives a complete list of these in a famous gloss.[3] In one or two cases, the second century teacher, R. Meir, who was a scribe by profession, had different readings from the established[4] text. And the Rabbis speak of three scrolls in the Temple courtyard, with alternative readings in certain verses.[5] As for the passage in the Creed we have noted,

[1] Ex. xvii. 15–16. [2] Deut. xxxi. i. [3] Sabb. 55b.
[4] B.R. ix; B.R. xx; B.R. xciv. though these may be no more than marginal glosses, as W. Bacher suggested, and not textual emendations.
[5] Yer. Ta'an. 68a.

the well-known Yigdal hymn, also part of the liturgy, formulates this principle in far less emphatic terms so as to leave room for the permissibility of textual criticism:

The Creedal Form	The Yigdal Form
I believe with perfect faith that the whole Torah, now in our possession, is the same that was given to Moses our Teacher, peace be unto him.[1]	Through him (Moses), the faithful in His house, the Lord The law of truth to Israel did accord.[2]

So that there is really nothing to deter the faithful Jew from accepting the principle of textual criticism. This does not, of course, mean that Jews who are convinced of the correctness of a textual variant should proceed to alter the Scroll in the Synagogue. (It is said that when the historian Graetz visited England for the Anglo-Jewish Historical Exhibition in the last century and he was called to the reading of the Haftarah, he read this according to his own amended version!). For the traditional text has acquired, as it were, a life of its own and the interpretations to which it has given rise possess a value that is independent of the actual meaning of the text. For example, in the instances quoted above, the validity of the rabbinic interpretation that the throne of God is incomplete as long as Amelek, the symbol of wanton brutality, exists, or the beauty of the rabbinic notion that God finished His work on the *seventh* day because rest itself is a creation, are in no way affected even if we prefer the readings of *nes*, instead of *kes*, and the *sixth* day, instead of the *seventh* day. Similarly, although the translation: 'In all their afflictions He was afflicted',[3] is based on a dubious text (the Septuagint reading is preferable), the idea it expresses that God suffers with man has become so important a part of Jewish thinking on the problem of pain that to alter the text for the purpose of reading in the Synagogue would be an act of spiritual vandalism. The interpretation has now become as much part of the Torah—in the third sense of the word noted above—as the text itself.

[1] Singer's Prayer Book, p. 90.
[2] Singer's, p. 2.
[3] Is. lxiii. 9.

But if to resort to textual criticism is not to offend against the doctrine of 'Torah from Heaven', we are on admittedly more dangerous ground when considering what is now known as the Higher Criticism, in which the traditional views concerning the authorship of the Biblical books is seriously contested.

During the Middle Ages, the only people to cast doubts on the Mosaic authorship of the Pentateuch were the heretics who were recognised as such. However, Abraham Ibn Ezra (1092–1167) (an 'orthodox' scholar whose commentary is always included in the better editions of the rabbinic Bible) appears to question this view. The passage under discussion is a cryptic one and is not easily deciphered, but this is its meaning according to Spinoza: In the verse: 'These are the words which Moses spoke unto all Israel beyond the Jordan'[1] the words 'beyond the Jordan' are puzzling. In Moses' day the Israelites had not yet entered Palestine so that in those days the words 'beyond the Jordan' would refer to Palestine itself, not to the land in which the Israelites were encamped when they heard Moses' farewell address. On this Ibn Ezra says. 'If you know the secret of the twelve, and of "And Moses wrote", "And the Canaanite was then in the land", "Behold his bedstead was a bedstead of iron" you will discover the truth'. Spinoza, in his *Theological and Political Tract*, published in 1670, explained this as follows. 'The secret of the twelve' means the last twelve verses of the Pentateuch which deal with the death of Moses and could not have been written by Moses himself. Similarly, the words 'And Moses wrote'[2] presuppose another author. 'And the Canaanite was *then* in the land'[3] is hard to explain if this verse were written by Moses because in his day they were still in the land. 'Behold his bedstead was a bedstead of iron'[4] speaks of the bedstead of Og, king of Bashan, who was slain by Moses near the end of the latter's life, while the words appear to suggest that the bedstead was pointed out as a landmark many years after Og had been slain. Ibn Ezra's comment has been interpreted in more

[1] Deut. i. 1.
[2] Ex. xxiv. 4, Num. xxxiii. 2, Deut. xxxi. 9.
[3] Gen. xii. 6.
[4] Deut. iii. 11.

orthodox fashion but if Spinoza is right this mediaeval thinker was the forerunner of Biblical criticism. Spinoza himself thinks that the Pentateuch was compiled in the days of Ezra.

The next step was the publication in 1753 of Jean Astruc's *Conjectures sur les memoires originaux dont il paroit que Moyse se servit pour composer le livre de la Genèse*. Astruc, a professor at the University of Paris, argued in favour of the Mosaic authorship of the Pentateuch, but suggested that Moses made use of various sources in compiling the book of Genesis. He conjectured that the two divine names—*Elohim* (translated in English as 'God') and the Tetragrammaton, *YHWH* (translated as 'Lord')—were used by two different sources. Following Astruc, other scholars developed what is now known as the Documentary Hypothesis. Eichorn tried to show that these two sources differed not alone in their use of the divine names but also in their style and vocabulary. Ewald carried the analysis of sources into the other books of the Pentateuch, and Graf and Wellhausen tried to demonstrate the chronological order of the various sources. As a result of these researches the Documentary Hypothesis thinks of four distinct sources—the Elohist (which uses the divine name *Elohim*), known as *E;* the *J* source (after the German spelling of *YHWH* with a *J*); the Priestly Code, said to have been produced in priestly circles and known as *P;* and the book of Deuteronomy identified with the Book of the Law found in the time of Josiah,[1] and known as *D*. It is further suggested that the book of Joshua is part of the same literary unit as the Pentateuch, hence the term Hextateuch. It is claimed that these four sources J.E.P.D. were fused together by an editor or editors.

Bible Criticism does not, of course limit itself to the Pentateuch. It critically examines the traditional view concerning the authorship of the other Biblical books. Thus, on linguistic, historical and literary grounds, the critics reject the Davidic authorship of Psalms, the Solomonic authorship of the Song of Songs, Proverbs and Ecclesiastes, and the authorship by Isaiah of the second part of the book which bears his name. It must also here be pointed out that in addition to literary analysis

[1] II Kings xxii and xxiii.

modern criticism avails itself of archaeological discoveries, such as the monuments and literature of the Assyrians, Babylonians, Egyptians and the Canaanites, and Comparative Religion in attempting to reconstruct the early religion and history of Israel. It is beyond the scope of this book to do more than briefly sketch the critical view. For more detailed information the reader must go to the numerous Introductions to the Bible and the articles in such works as Hasting's *Dictionary of the Bible* and the *Jewish Encyclopedia.*

The following is Maimonides' statement of the eighth principle of the Jewish Faith: [1] *'That the Torah has been revealed from heaven.* This implies our belief that the whole of the Torah found in our hands this day is the Torah that was handed down by Moses and that is all of divine origin. By this I mean that the whole of the Torah came to him from before God in a manner which is metaphorically called "speaking"; but the real nature of that communication is unknown to everybody except to Moses (peace to him!) to whom it came. In handing down the Torah, Moses was like a scribe writing from dictation the whole of it, its chronicles, its narratives, and its precepts. It is in this sense that he is termed *mehokek* (=copyist).[2] And there is no difference between verses like "And the sons of Ham were Cush and Mizraim, Phut and Canaan",[3] or "And his wife's name was Mehetabel, the daughter of Matred"[4] or "And Timna was concubine",[5] and verses like "I am the Lord thy God"[6] and "Hear, O Israel".[7] They are all equally of divine origin and all belong to the "Law of God which is perfect, pure, holy, and true". In the opinion of the Rabbins, Manassah was the most renegade and the greatest of all infidels because he thought that in the Torah there was a kernel and a husk, and that these histories and anecdotes have no value and emanate from Moses. This is the significance of the expression "The Torah does not come

[1] Trans. of J. Abelson in J.Q.R. (O.S.) Vol. XIX, 1907, p. 24f.
[2] This is better than Abelson's translation as 'lawgiver'.
[3] Gen. x. 6.
[4] Gen. xxxvi. 39.
[5] Gen. xxxvi. 12.
[6] Ex. xx. 2.
[7] Deut. vi. 4.

from heaven", which, say the Rabbins, is the remark of one who believes that all the Torah is of divine origin save a certain verse which (says he) was not spoken by God but by Moses himself. And of such a one the verse says "For he hath despised the word of the Lord".[1] May God be exalted far above and beyond the speech of the Infidels! For truly in every letter of the Torah there reside wise maxims and admirable truths for him to whom God has given understanding. You cannot grasp the uttermost bounds of its wisdom. "It is larger in measure than the earth, and wider than the sea".[2] Man has but to follow in the footsteps of the anointed one of the God of Jacob, who prayed "Open my eyes and I shall behold wonderful things from Thy Law". The interpretation of traditional law is in like manner of divine origin. And that which we know today of the nature of Succah, Lulab, Shofar, Fringes and Phylacteries is essentially the same as that which God commanded Moses, and which the latter told us. In the success of his mission Moses realised the mission of a *ne'emon* "a faithful servant of God".[3] The text in which the eighth principle of faith is indicated is: "Hereby ye shall know that the Lord hath sent me to do all these words; for I have not done them of mine own mind".[4]

This view of Maimonides—the dominant one until recent times—is obviously at variance with critical theories and those who accept it must perforce look upon the latter as negative and destructive of faith. To talk about 'reconciling' the Maimonidean idea and the Documentary Hypothesis (or, for that matter, any other view based on 'untraditional' methods of investigation) is futile for you cannot reconcile two contradictory theories. But to say this is not to preclude the possibility of a *synthesis* between the old and new knowledge. There is a clear distinction between saying that two points of view are both correct and saying that they both *contain* truth. There is a delightful Jewish anecdote about a married couple who complained to a Rabbi that they were unable to get

[1] Num. xv. 31.
[2] Job. xi. 9.
[3] Num. xii. 7.
[4] Num. xvi. 28

along together. The Rabbi heard the plea of the husband and said: 'My son, you are right'. He then heard the plea of the wife and said: 'My daughter, you are right'. when his wife questioned: 'How can they both be right?', the Rabbi replied: 'My dear, you are also right'! And yet every marriage guidance counsellor will testify that there is generally right on both sides in marital disputes. The problem is this—are we compelled either to turn our backs on all criticism or dismiss over two thousand years of Jewish tradition and interpretation? Or can a synthesis be found? This we shall consider in the next chapter.

CHAPTER VII

A Synthesis of the Traditional and Critical Views

THREE distinct attitudes are possible with regard to the challenge of Bible Criticism and its implications for Jewish observance, and each of these has found protagonists among Jews in this century. There is the school which accepts the critical position more or less *in toto* to the detriment not alone of the doctrine of 'Torah from Heaven' but also to the practical observances of Judaism. Another school feels obliged to reject entirely, and to combat positively in the name of Orthodoxy, any untraditional views. And there is the third view according to which a synthesis between the traditional and critical theories is possible and that, in any event, the attitude of respect, reverence and obedience *vis-à-vis* Jewish observance is not radically affected by an 'untraditional' outlook on questions of Biblical authorship and composition.

Most thinkers of the Reform school, nowadays, adopt, more or less, the full critical position and draw from it what appears to them to be the logical conclusion that the ritual precepts of the Pentateuch are no longer binding upon Jews, not having been given by God to Moses. The lofty ethical standards of the Bible and the principles of justice, righteousness and holiness are binding because of their basic truth and their appeal to man's higher nature.

The second view is that of such Orthodox scholars as David Hoffmann (1843–1921), the author of the brilliant *Die wichtigsten Instanzen gegen die Graf-Wellhausensche Hypothese*. Hoffman attacks the critics with great acumen and tremendous erudition on their own ground and with their own methods. But it is not without significance that Hoffman himself was the originator of what has been called 'The Higher Criticism of the Mishnah', in which the great Code of Jewish law is subjected to exactly the same kind of literary analysis— various 'strata', redactors and all—which the critics use in their investigations into the Biblical literature. As Hoffman in fact declares, his opposition to the Higher Criticism is on grounds of *faith*. As an orthodox Jew he feels compelled to reject the critical position as erroneous and he then uses his considerable skill in demolishing the edifice the critics have so laboriously erected.

Dr. J. H. Hertz, the late Chief Rabbi of the British Empire, was one of the most determined opponents of the critical theory, calling the Graf-Wellhausen hypothesis a perversion of history and a desecration of religion. Dr. Hertz devotes a large portion of his famous commentary to the *Humash* to attacking the Higher Criticism. Typical of his remarks in this connection is the following: 'The procedure of the critics in connection with the Creation and Deluge chapters is typical of their method throughout. It justifies the protest of the late Lord Chancellor of England, the Earl of Halsbury—an excellent judge of evidence—who in 1915 found himself impelled to declare: "For my own part I consider the assignment of different fragments of Genesis to a number of wholly imaginary authors, great rubbish. I do not understand the attitude of those men who base a whole theory of this kind on hypotheses for which there is no evidence whatsoever". A generation before the Earl of Halsbury, the historian Lecky gave expression to a similar judgment, in the following words: "I may be pardoned for expressing my belief that this kind of investigation is often pursued with an exaggerated confidence. Plausible conjecture is too easily mistaken for positive proof. Undue significance is attached to what may be mere casual coincidence, and a minuteness of accuracy is professed in discriminating between different elements in a narrative which cannot be attained by mere internal evidence".'[1]

Many modern scholars without any theological bias reject the hypothesis on purely scientific grounds. The Uppsala School, Umberto Cassutto, Ezekiel Kaufmann and others have all suggested alternative theories, though none of these is in complete accord with the traditional view, Professor Cassutto,[2] for

[1] By far the best and most effective critique of the Documentary Hypothesis in English is that of Solomon Goldman in his *In the Beginning*, to which the reader is referred. N.Y., 1941, p. 77f. Cf. the same author's *The Book of Books, An Introduction*, Phil., 1948.

[2] *The Documentary Hypothesis* (Hebrew), Sec. Ed., Jer. 1953.

example, takes each of the five pillars on which the Documentary Hypothesis stands—the different divine names, the differences in style and language, contradictions between two passages, repetitions in two passages, and the combination of two accounts—and demonstrates that they have been set up by scholars incapable of appreciating the niceties of ancient Hebrew style and linguistic distinctions. To give but one example, the expressions 'going out of Egypt' and 'going *up* out of Egypt' are not at all due to different sources, each with its own idiom, but they represent the expressions of the same 'source' for two different things—the one refers to the Exodus alone, the other to the whole journey of the Israelites from Egypt to the Promised Land. But Cassutto recognises—and here we arrive at the third point of view—that unfounded though the Documentary Hypothesis is, the question is a *literary* one, not a religious question. 'We must approach this task', writes Cassutto, 'with complete objectivity, without any sort of preconception in favour of one school or another. We must be ready from the beginning of our investigation to accept its results wherever they may lead. And there is no need for us to be alarmed for the honour of our Torah and its holiness. The honour of our Torah and its holiness are above the realm of literary criticism, they depend on the inner content of the books of the Torah and are in no way dependent on the solution of literary problems which have to do merely with the external form, with the "language of men" in which, as the Rabbis say, the Torah speaks. . . .'[1] *This, in fact, is the fundamental question—not whether this or that theory is correct, but whether the appeal to tradition is valid in matters to which the normal canons of historical and literary method apply, and whether the authority of Jewish Law is weakened as a result of scientific investigation.* The third view holds that we can afford to be objective in examining the literary problems of the Bible and that it does not at all follow that because, as a result of more highly developed methods of investigation, including the use of archaeological evidence, we are compelled to adopt different views from the ancients, we must automatically give up the rich and spiritually satisfying tradition that

[1] *Ibid.*, pp. 16–17.

has been built up with devotion and self-sacrifice by the wisest and best of Jews.

This third view is finding an increasing number of adherents. The historical school argues that literary problems can only be solved by the use of those methods which have been applied so successfully in the examination of other documents of antiquity—the Greek and Latin classics, for example. Its members will keep an open mind on many of the problems, realising that after so many centuries many of the difficulties never will be solved. But this approach in no way invalidates the observance of jewish practices. These derive their authority from the undeniable fact that they have provided Jews with 'ladders to heaven' and still have the power of sanctifying Jewish life in accordance with the Jewish ideal; because of this we recognise that it was God who gave them and it is His will that we obey when we submit to the Torah discipline. As Franz Rosenzweig has so finely put it: 'Where we differ from orthodoxy is in our reluctance to draw from our belief in the holiness or uniqueness of the Torah, and in its character of revelation, any conclusions as to its literary genesis and the philological value of the text as it has come down to us. If all of Wellhausen's theories were correct and the Samaritans really had the better text, our faith would not be shaken in the least'.[1]

One of the most original thinkers among the Rabbis of the older school, Rabbi Hayyim Hirschenson, wrote some years ago a fascinating Responsum on the Jewish attitude to Bible Criticism. Hirschenson, who was asked if Bible Criticism may be taught at the Hebrew University, endeavoured to apply Halachic method to the problem. The Halachah knows of three categories with regard to liability—these are, *hayyabh*, 'obligation', i.e. the incurment of a penalty; *patur* 'exemption' but *assur* 'forbidden', i.e. though there is no penalty for the offence there is prohibition; and *patur* and *muttar*, 'exempt and permitted', i.e. not only is there no penalty but there is no prohibition. With regard to Sabbath law, for instance, work prohibited in the Bible involves the full penalty of Sabbath desecration; work forbidden by rabbinic law is pro-

[1] *Franz Rosenzweig—His Life and Thought*, N.Y., 1953, p. 158.

hibited but there is no penalty attached to the prohibition; and there are certain forms of work involving no prohibition whatsoever. Hirschenson suggests[1] that the main objection in the Talmudic sources to the rejection of the doctrine of 'Torah from Heaven' is that such a rejection impugns the honesty of Moses by suggesting that he wrote something he had not received from God. The *hayyabh* offence in this field, for which the penalty of exclusion from the World to Come is incurred, is the denigration of Moses' character in maintaining that he wilfully forged the Biblical documents. On the other hand, the study of textual criticism is both *patur* and *muttar*, for, as we have seen, such criticism was at times resorted to in the Talmudic age. Modern Bible Criticism does not suggest that Moses forged the documents but that they are not the work of Moses at all. This, because it is in opposition to the established traditions of our people, is *assur* 'forbidden', but not *hayyabh*. Hence, Hirschenson concludes it would not be necessary for the orthodox Jew to boycott the Hebrew University because some of its Professors espouse the cause of Higher Criticism.

Hirschenson's view as it stands is hardly historical. It is, to say the least, unlikely that the chief purpose of those who so zealously fought on behalf of the doctrine of 'Torah from Heaven' was to safeguard the reputation of Moses. But accepting his adoption of Halachic categories we can say much for the view that present-day criticism would not fall under the complete *hayyabh* ban of the Rabbis. The chief concern of the Rabbis was not with questions of authorship but of inspiration. Is the Torah the word of God? This was the concern of the ancient teachers. In Talmudic times, no one, not even the heretic, doubted that the Torah was written by Moses. Hence, in those days the fundamental question was did Moses write it of his own accord or under divine inspiration? Even if the most radical theories of the critics are accepted this means no more than that the base of the problem has been shifted, but the question of the divine origin of the Torah is not radically affected. An excellent illustration of this is the Talmudic debates on whether the book of Ecclesiastes

[1] *Malki Ba-Kodesh*, Vol. I and II, St. Louis, 1919-1921.

is to be admitted into the Canon of Holy Writ. Those who would admit it argue that Solomon wrote it under the influence of the divine spirit. Those who oppose its admission argue that it is the product of 'Solomon's wisdom', i.e. the fruit of his own, uninspired thinking.[1] In other words the Solomonic authorship of the book was accepted by everyone; the only question to be considered was, is the book so inspired as to merit inclusion in the Canon? Now that all scholars are unanimous in rejecting the Solomonic authorship of the book, there is still no reason for rejecting the opinion that it is worthy of inclusion in the Canon on account of its inspiration.

There is much too in the suggestion that the Rabbis had a sound polemical motive in emphasizing that the whole of the Torah was given 'at once' to Moses. They were chiefly concerned with a rebuttal of the Christian view that the Torah was a temporary institution, that there had been a 'progressive revelation' and that, therefore, the 'New Testament' could be looked upon as a culmination of the 'Old'.[2] Students of the Talmudic and Midrashic literature will recall many such examples of religious polemic, consciously erring on the side of anachronism, in order to make its point clear. A good example of this is the oft-repeated Rabbinic teaching that Abraham kept the whole of the Torah before it was given—in contradistinction to the Christian view that it was not necessary to keep the Torah in order to lead the good life.[3]

Dr. J. Abelson has thus stated the third view of which we have spoken. 'The correct perspective of the matter seems to be as follows: the modern criticism of the Bible on the one hand, and faith in Judaism on the other hand, can be regarded as two distinct compartments. For criticism, even at its best, is speculative and tentative, something always liable to be modified or proved wrong and having to be replaced by something else. It is an intellectual exercise, subject to all the doubts and guesses which are inseparable from such exercises. But our accredited truths of Judaism have their foundations more

[1] Tos. Yad. II; Meg. 7a.
[2] See Bernard J. Bamberger: *Revelations of the Torah After Sinai*, in Hebrew Union College Annual, Vol. XVI, 1941, p. 97f.
[3] See Ginzberg's *Legends of the Jews*, Vol. V, p. 259, n. 275.

deeply and strongly laid than all this. And our faith in them not only need be uninjured by our faith in criticism, but need not be affected by the latter at all. The two are quite consistent and can be held simultaneously. I can quite understand any one talking as follows: I like the Higher Criticism, I study it, I appreciate much of its teaching and its general sentiment, I fancy that much in Judaism can be brought into line with it, I think that it may be in accordance with truth and it may not be in accordance with truth, and therefore I sit on the hedge; as to my notions of the basic truths of Judaism, my reading in criticism has not changed them one bit. The one is airy, floating intellectualism, the other is consolidated religion. They lie in different spheres and have no necessary bearing one on the other'.[1]

A somewhat different, but similarly helpful, view is expounded by Will Herberg,[2] claiming to follow Rosenzweig, Buber, Neibuhr and Brunner. In this view, both modernism and fundamentalism are wrong in insisting that our concept of revelation must be either one or the other. The third way is not 'between' modernism and fundamentalism but beyond and distinct from both, so that those who tread this way may take Scripture with the utmost seriousness as the record of revelation while avoiding the pitfalls of fundamentalism. As Herberg puts it: 'In this view, a shift in the very meaning of the term "revelation" is involved. Revelation is not the communication of infallible information, as the fundamentalists claim, nor is it the outpouring of "inspired" sages and poets, as the modernists conceive it. Revelation is the *self-disclosure of God in his dealings with the world*. Scripture is thus not itself revelation but a humanly mediated record of revelation. It is a story composed of many strands and fragments, each arising in its own time, place and circumstances, yet it is essentially one, for it is throughout the story of the encounter of God and man in the history of Israel. Scripture as revelation is not a compendium of recondite information or metaphysical propositions; it is quite literally *Heilsgeschichte*, redemptive history'.

---

[1] 'Bible Problems and Modern Knowledge', in *The Jewish Review*, March, 1913, p. 483. The whole article is well worth careful study.
[2] *Judaism and Modern Man*, p. 243f.

It goes without saying that these or similar views which see no incompatibility between the idea of Scripture as the Word of God and the use of critical *methods* in its investigation, can only be entertained if the doctrine of 'verbal' inspiration is rejected. It is true that in the vast range of Jewish teaching on revelation there are numerous passages in which 'verbal' inspiration is accepted or, at least, hinted at. But this is not the whole story. It can be demonstrated that long before the rise of modern criticism some of the Jewish teachers had a conception of revelation which leaves room for the idea of human co-operation with the divine. It will be helpful if a few of the passages containing these ideas are quoted.

(1) The Talmud[1] tells of an oven, the ritual purity of which is debated by R. Eliezer (2nd Cent. C.E.) and the sages. R. Eliezer said to the Sages: If the ruling is as I hold let this carob-tree prove it. Thereupon the carob-tree was torn out of its place but the Sages retorted: No proof can be brought from a carob-tree. R. Eliezer then said: If the ruling accords with me, let the stream of water prove it. Whereupon the stream flowed backwards but the Sages said: No proof can be brought from a stream of water. Again R. Eliezer urged: Let the walls of the House of Learning prove it. Whereupon the walls of the House of Learning began to totter but the Sages remained unconvinced. Finally, R. Eliezer said: If I am right let it be proved from Heaven, and a Heavenly voice cried out: Why do you dispute with R. Eliezer, seeing that in all matters the law is in accord with his ruling? But R. Joshua said: 'It is not in Heaven'[2]—the Torah states 'After the majority must one incline'[3] and this means that the law must be decided by a majority of human judges and no appeal to a heavenly voice is valid. The story concludes that when R. Nathan met Elijah, the Prophet, he asked him: What did the Holy One blessed be He do in that hour? And the answer was that He laughed with joy, saying, 'My sons have defeated Me, My sons have defeated Me'!

(2) They were disputing in the Heavenly Academy: If the bright spot preceded the white hair,[4] he is unclean; if the re-

---

[1] B.M. 59b.   [3] Ex. xxiii. 2.
[2] Deut. xxx. 12   [4] See Lev. xiii. 1–3.

verse he is clean. If in doubt—the Holy One, blessed be He, ruled, clean, the entire Heavenly Academy ruled, He is unclean. They asked: Who shall decide it? Rabbah bar Nahmani, for he is a great authority on these matters. Rabbah died and as he died he exclaimed, 'Clean, clean!'[1]

(3) R. Isaac said: The same watchword (communication) is revealed to many prophets, yet no two prophets prophecy in the identical phraseology, if they are true prophets.[2] An anticipation of the recognition by modern scholars that the prophetic inspiration is mediated through the personality of the prophet; Amos speaking in the language of a herdsman, Isaiah in the language of a prince.

(4) Isaiah and Ezekiel both saw the King, say the Rabbis,[3] but Isaiah as a city-dweller, familiar with the sight of the king and his court, hence his description is brief, Ezekiel as a rustic who is filled with wonder at the unfamiliar sight, hence his description is lengthy.

(5) Rab Judah said in the name of Rab, when Moses ascended on high he found the Holy One, blessed be He, engaged in fixing crowns to the letters of the Torah. Moses asked after the meaning of these crowns and God told him that there will arise a man, at the end of many generations, Akiba ben Joseph by name, who will expound upon each tittle heaps and heaps of laws. 'Lord of the Universe', said Moses, 'permit me to see him'. God replied: 'Turn thee round'. Moses went and sat behind eight rows of Akiba's disciples. Not being able to follow their discussions he was ill at ease, but when they came to a certain subject and the disciples said to the master: 'Whence do you know it?' and the latter replied: 'It is a law given to Moses on Sinai,' he was comforted. Thereupon he returned to the Holy One, blessed be He, and said: 'Lord of the Universe, Thou hast such a man and Thou givest the Torah by me!'[4] He replied, 'Be silent, for so it has come to My mind'. In other words the Torah that Akiba was teaching was so different from the Torah given to Moses—because the social, economic, political and religious conditions were so different in Akiba's day—that, at first, Moses could not recognise his Torah in the Torah

[1] B.M. 86a.
[2] Sanh. 89a.
[3] Hag. 13b.
[4] Men. 29b.

taught by Akiba. But he was reassured when he realised that Akiba's Torah was *implicit* in his Torah, was, indeed, an attempt to make his Torah relevant to the spiritual needs of Jews in the age of Akiba.

(6) R. Ishmael b. Elisha (1st-2nd Cent. C.E.) disagreed with those of his contemporaries who derived rules and teachings from a pleonastic word or syllable, e.g. the use of the infinite absolute form of the verb. For instance, the verse concerning idolators in which it is said that they 'will *surely* be cut off'—*hikkareth tikkareth*[1]—is interpreted by Akiba to convey the thought that they will be cut off in both this world and the next. To this Ishmael replied that no teachings can be derived from such expressions for this is how Hebrew was spoken and 'the Torah speaks in the language of men'![2]

It is well known that Maimonides used this principle to explain the Biblical anthropomorphisms.[3]

(7) When a Rabbinic precept is carried out, e.g. the kindling of the Hannukah lights, the blessing to be recited runs: 'Who hast sanctified us with His commandments and *hast commanded* us to . . .'[4] In other words, not only did the Rabbis recognise a human element in the Bible, they perceived the divine in post-Biblical developments of Judaism.

(8) Azariah Figo (1579-1647) gives this interpretation to the rabbinic distinction between Moses and other prophets, that he saw God through a polished glass while they saw Him through a dim glass. Moses saw God Himself, as if through a window pane; the other prophets saw only His image as reflected in a mirror, i.e. through their own personalities,[5] as we would say. Figo's view goes further than the Rabbinic views mentioned above (3 and 4). The Rabbis speak of the prophets seeing God and *expressing* what they had seen through their personalities; Figo speaks of the prophets *seeing* God through their own personalities!

[1] Num. xv. 31.
[2] Sifre Num. 15. 31; Yer. Yeb. viii, 8d; Yer. Ned. i. 36c; B.M. 31b and freq. see J.E. Vol. VI, p. 649.
[3] Guide, Part I, Chapter xxvi. Cf. Bahya: 'Duties of the Heart,' *Sha'ar Ha-Yihud*, Chapter 10.
[4] See Sabb. 23a.
[5] *Binnah Le-'Ittim*, P. II, Ser. 44, quoted by Israel Bettan, Studies in Jewish Preaching, Cincinatti, 1939, p. 255–256.

(9) Isaac of Vorka (a famous Hasidic Rabbi) said: It is told in the Midrash: The Ministering angels once said to God: 'You have permitted Moses to write whatever he wants to, so there is nothing to prevent him from saying to Israel: I have given you the Torah'. God replied: 'This he would not do, but if he did he would still be keeping faith with me'. The Rabbi interpreted this with a parable. A merchant wanted to go on a journey. He took an assistant and let him work in his shop. He himself spent most of his time in the adjoining room from where he could hear what was going on next door. During the first few weeks he sometimes heard his assistant tell a customer 'The master cannot let this go for so low a price'. The merchant did not go on his journey. During the next few weeks he occasionally heard the voice next door say: 'We cannot let it go for so low a price'. He still postponed his journey. But in the next few weeks he heard the assistant say: 'I cannot let it go for so low a price'. It was then that he started on his journey.[1]

(10) The rival schools of Hillel and Shammai debated, we are told, for a number of years, whose ruling should be accepted. Eventually a Heavenly voice proclaimed: 'The words of both are the words of the living God, but the rule is in accordance with the school of Hillel'[2]—another example of Rabbinic recognition of the divine in post-Biblical developments.

Allowing for the legendary nature of some of the above passages, it must be obvious that many Jewish teachers conceived of revelation in more dynamic terms than the doctrine of 'verbal' inspiration would imply. For them, revelation is an encounter between the divine and the human, so that there is a human as well as a divine factor in revelation, God revealing His Will not alone to men but *through* men. No doubt our new attitude to the Biblical record, in which, as the result of historical, literary and archaeological investigations, the Bible is seen against the background of the times in which its various books were written, ascribes more to the human element than the ancients would have done, but this is a difference in degree, not in kind. The new knowledge need not in any way affect our reverence for the Bible and our loyalty to its teachings. God's

[1] Buber: *Tales of the Hasidim, The Later Masters*, N.Y., 1948, p. 295–6.
[2] Erub. 13b.

Power is not lessened because He preferred to co-operate with His creatures in producing the Book of Books. Applying his words to our problem, we can fittingly quote the penetrating observation of the ancient Talmudic sage, that in every passage in the Bible where the greatness of God is mentioned, there you find also His humility.[1]

This chapter might suitably be concluded with the splendid illustration of the point of view we have been trying to sketch, given by Emil Brunner. Brunner asks us to think of a gramophone record. The voice we hear on the record is the voice we want to hear, it is the actual voice of the artist who delights us, but we hear it through the inevitable distortions of the record. We hear the authentic voice of God speaking to us through the pages of the Bible—we know that it is the voice of God because of the uniqueness of its message and the response it awakens in our higher nature—and its truth is in no way affected in that we can only hear that voice through the medium of human beings who, hearing it for the first time, endeavoured to record it for us.

[1] Meg. 31a.

CHAPTER VIII

Bible Difficulties

IF the view of the Biblical record sketched above is acceptable, it frees us from the harrowing doubts concerning those inaccuracies and inferior moral ideas found in the Bible, known as Bible 'difficulties'. For if the Bible, though the Word of God, is the product of the divine co-operating with the human, then human imperfection will be found in it side by side with divine perfection. As has been said in this connection, the setting of a pearl of great price is not part of the pearl, the precious jewel shines with its own light (Dean Matthews). There are two kinds of difficulties, which we proceed to examine, the scientific and the moral.

(1) *Scientific Difficulties.*

Most educated people today accept the picture of the age of the earth, the size of the universe, and the early history of man, revealed by modern science, even though this differs from the account of these things which emerges from a literal reading of the Biblical books. especially of the book of Genesis. Twentieth century Jewish apologetics does not feel obliged to combat the new knowledge in the name of the Lord. Even so orthodox a thinker as the ate Rav Kook could have said that the evolutionary hypothesis, far from being at variance with the Jewish outlook, is in full accord with the Kabbalistic view of the whole of creation slowly climbing to ever greater heights, and that the early chapters of Genesis were always understood as belonging to the 'secrets of the Torah' so that a literal reading of them was ruled out of court.[1]

Present-day religious thinkers who deal with this problem

[1] See M. M. Kasher in *Talpioth*, N.Y., Vol. VI, 1953, p. 205f and I. Epstein: *The Faith of Judaism*, 1954, p. 194f.

frequently write that the Bible is not a scientific text-book but a work of guidance and inspiration in the realm of religion and morals and we must not expect its opinions on scientific matters to be 'up to date'. But valid though this is, it requires some elaboration. After all, it may be argued, how can a divinely inspired work be inaccurate in matters of fact? The answer to this is, if eternal truth is to be revealed to man and expressed in his language so that he can grasp its substance, it can only be transmitted in a manner which reflects the thought-patterns of the age in which the revelation takes place. The prophet comforts his people by assuring them that God cares and He will lead them back to the land of their fathers 'from the four corners of the earth'. Is the power, the truth and the beauty of his message in any way affected by the fact that he thought, as all men did in his day, that the earth was flat? It is no part of the belief in prophecy, of faith in the divine message contained in the books of the Prophets, that God in some miraculous manner gave the prophets such incidental information about the physical universe to enable them to know, many centuries before this was discovered by the normal application of reason after a long process of scientific development, that the earth was round.

A recent non-Jewish writer has put it in this way: 'To make this clearer. Suppose we gave the Bible to a committee of highest scientific experts today and told them so to change and remodel every phrase therein touching on scientific matters as to bring it in line with the very latest stage of the physical sciences. Such a corrected Bible would probably be utterly out of date in one generation, and if again corrected, it would again be out of date in a further generation. If God, in inspiring human authors wished them to remain human and wished to be understood, God would naturally use speech betraying the limitations of the human mind at the time of writing, unless indeed He directly and miraculously revealed further scientific truth. But the purpose of the Bible is not to further scientific discovery, its purpose is to teach men the way to go to heaven, not the way the heavens go. In consequence, no one should marvel or think it unworthy of God that it is plain that the human authors of the Bible knew no more of scientific matters than their contemporaries did, and less even than what the man in the street knows today'.[1]

One who reads his Bible in the spirit of reverence for the Word of God and respect for human reason, soon learns to distinguish between the eternal and the ephemeral in its pages. He soon sees that even those passages which use the language of a bygone age are still shot through with the kind of penetrating insight into reality than can only be explained in transcendental terms. To give but one example. The Genesis story of creation uses the Hebrew word *bara*, 'to create', of three things. Of the creation of matter: 'In the beginning God created (*bara*) the heavens and the earth';[2] of the creation of animal life: 'And God created (*bara*) great whales, and every living creature that moveth . . .'[3] and of the creation of human life: 'So God created (*bara*) man in his own image, in the image of God created he him . . .'[4] Now, there is a subtle difference in Hebrew between the word *bara* and the word of similar meaning *yatzar*. The former means 'to create'; the latter, also used in Genesis, means 'to fashion'. *Yatzar* is used of God 'fashioning' that which was already in existence. *Bara* is used of *creatio ex nihilo*, of God bringing into being that which did not before exist. This is not fanciful homiletics; it belongs to the correct understanding of the way the ancient Hebrews used their language. And by using the word *bara* of these three things, the narrative implies that only by believing in God can the emergence of matter, of life, and of the human spirit be explained. What is this matter about which we know today so much and yet so little? How did it come into being? Can we believe that it just 'happened'? The Theistic view is 'God created'—*bara*. And what of life? What was it that enabled life to emerge where there was formerly inert matter? How did the amoeba begin its slow climb to the higher forms of animal life from the mud and the slime of the prehistoric vastnesses? Again Theism answers: 'God created'—*bara*. And, finally, the soul of man! Granted man's animal ancestry, why is man different from the brute in kind,

---

[1] Canon Arendzen in *Religion and Science*, ed. C. Lattery, Lond., 1940, p. 214.
[2] Gen. i. 1.
[3] Gen. i. 21.
[4] Gen. i. 27.

not alone in degree? How explain the transformation of animality into rationality? How explain man's power to see visions, to dream dreams, to create beauty, to know truth, to embrace goodness? How explain the leap from the ape to man? Once again the glorious refrain replies 'God created'—*bara*.[1]

It is by no means irrelevant to remark that Judaism is far better equipped to deal with this problem than is Christianity. There are, on the whole, three reasons, none of which apply to Judaism, why Christian teachers in the last century felt obliged to wage the war of the Lord against science in defence of a literal interpretation of Genesis, and why, basically, fundamentalism is more acceptable to Christians than to Jews. First, the doctrine of the Fall of Man, based, of course, on the Adam and Eve story, occupies a far more prominent place in Christian than in Jewish theology. The whole case for the need of a saviour to redeem mankind from the sin of Adam is weakened if the Paradise story is interpreted figuratively. Secondly, from the earliest times, 'Old Testament' verses were quoted by the Church as foretelling the birth and activity of Jesus, so that it was naturally felt that to question the literalness of any Biblical verse was to undermine the foundations of this whole method in interpretation. In the essay quoted above, Canon Arendzen states the view of his (the Catholic) Church in this way: 'It is possible that the account of the origin of woman in the Bible contains expressions which are metaphors and must not be taken quite literally, but the fact itself that the first woman came into being from man, is so universally regarded as *bound up with the doctrine of original sin, of the parallelism of Christ the Second Adam with the first Adam who fell, of the doctrine of the subordination of woman to man in I Corinthians XI, 8-9 and I Timothy II, 13* that the decision of the Biblical Commission (to take the story literally) seems but an echo of an unbroken tradition.' (*italics mine*). It would be exceedingly difficult to find a parallel to this kind of thinking in Jewish sources. Thirdly, according to the Gospels, Jesus himself appears to have accepted the 'fundamentalistic' interpretation of Scripture. Bishop Gore's suggestion that in his human nature he

[1] This passage was suggested by the remarks of Professor T. H. Robinson, in his Epilogue to *The Old Testament and Modern Study*, p. 351-2.

shared the erroneous views of his day, is sufficiently well-known! Nothing in the Jewish faith is basically affected by a non-literal interpretation of Genesis and, as Rav Kook has said, such interpretation was the norm long before the rise of modern science.

(2) *Moral Difficulties.*

We now turn to the moral difficulties and cite as an example one of the most perplexing, the extermination of the Canaanites. 'And Joshua turned back at that time, and took Hazor, and smote the king thereof with the sword; for Hazor before time was the head of all those kingdoms. And they smote all the souls that were therein with the edge of the sword, utterly destroying them; there was none left that breathed; and he burnt Hazor with fire. And all the cities of those kings, and all the kings of them, did Joshua take, and he smote them with the edge of the sword, and utterly destroyed them; as Moses the servant of the Lord commanded . . . And all the spoil of these cities, and the cattle, the children of Israel took for a prey unto themselves; but every man they smote with the edge of the sword, until they had destroyed them, neither left they any that breathed. As the Lord commanded Moses His servant so did Moses command Joshua; he left nothing undone of all that the Lord commanded Moses.'[1]

These and similar verses have long been a stumbling block in the path of faith in the Bible as the word of God. Those who rally to the defence of the Bible against the secularist onslaught with regard to the discrepancies between its views on the origin of the world and the picture revealed by modern science, have found refuge, as we have seen, in the perfectly sound argument that the Bible is not a scientific text-book but a guide to religion and morals. But what of the moral difficulties? What of such verses as those quoted which conflict with our ideas of right and wrong? If we would be horrified at the suggestion that after a successful war against our enemies we should utterly destroy them, how can we account for a description of such conduct, given with approval in a book in which we are expected to find guidance and inspiration?

[1] Josh. xi. 10–15.

It should first be noted that it is a perversion of the truth to compare, as Shaw did some years ago and as some do today, the destruction of the aboriginal savages inhabiting ancient Palestine with the ruthless Nazi extermination of the Jews in the twentieth century. For one thing the motive was entirely different. Whatever the faults of our people—and Jews have been the severest critics of their own shortcomings—it is now abundantly clear that hatred of Jewry was an integral part of the Nazi campaign against civilisation. 'Conscience is a Jewish invention' taunted the Nazis. Whereas, putting the very worst construction on the ancient story and refusing to gloss over the very real difficulties, the ancient Hebrews were bent on destroying cruel savages, whose foul practices included Moloch worship, in which infants were callously slaughtered to appease the anger of the gods and to buy their favours.

'When thou art come into the land which the Lord thy God giveth thee, thou shalt not learn to do after the abominations of those nations. There shall not be found among you any one that maketh his son or his daughter to pass through the fire, one that useth divination, a soothsayer, or an enchanter, or a sorcerer, or a charmer, or one that consulteth a ghost or a familiar spirit, or a necromancer. For whosoever doeth these things is an abomination unto the Lord; and because of these abominations the Lord thy God is driving them out before thee'.[1]

It is all too seldom realised that had the Israelites not conquered Palestine, Western civilisation may never have emerged from barbarism; that our moral ideas—including that which causes us to be shocked on reading the morally difficult passages in the Bible—are themselves the product of the Bible's influence.

This takes us to the heart of the problem. For so much depends on our attitude to that wonderful, yet at times puzzling, collection of books we call the Bible, and venerate as sacred literature. People who are shocked on reading the Biblical account of the extermination of the Canaanites usually have a crude conception of what is meant when it is claimed for the

[1] Deut. xviii. 9–12.

Bible that it is 'divinely inspired'. They take it to mean 'verbal' inspiration, that every word in the Bible was 'dictated' by God, and they fail to appreciate the human element of which we have spoken in the previous chapter. Dr. Hertz, in his excellent note on our problem, has this to say, among other things: 'Furthermore, the search for a new homeland, and the conquest of such homeland, are not isolated phenomena in World History. The fact is that the *population of nearly every European country today had conquered its present home-land and largely destroyed the original inhabitants.* Thus, the Saxons all but exterminated the Romanised Celts; and, in turn, the Saxons were 'harried' by the Normans on their conquest of England. Even more dreadful was the enslavement or extermination of the native races by both Catholic and Protestant settlers in their Overseas possessions. Now, no nation has ever been called upon to justify the taking of such lands, or its conduct towards the natives who passed under its control. The peoples exhaust the vocabulary of praise for those of its national heroes who secured that homeland or colonial possessions for them. Israel alone has such an ethical justification for the conquest of Canaan and the banning of its inhabitants.'[1] Why does this kind of apologetic leave us dissatisfied? Is it not that we expect a higher morality in the pages of the Bible than that of the Saxons and the Normans and even of the Catholic and Protestant settlers? We expect the Bible to be perfect. It is said that the head of the great Lithuanian Yeshiba of Telz, once defended his students against the accusation that they went for walks with girls. He admitted the fact but went on to say: 'But young men everywhere go for walks with girls so that the offence of my students appears to be that in addition they study the Torah'! Dr. Hertz's apology reminds us of this. All people have done it; why should Israel be the exception? But, it will be retorted, we expect Israel to be an exception and we expect the Torah of Israel to be free from the record of events that have disgraced other peoples.

But are we justified in demanding perfection in the Bible? Certainly, we are, if we understand the doctrine of revelation to mean verbal inspiration. But we have seen that in modern

[1] *Commentary to the Pentateuch*, Lond., 1938, p. 833.

times a different conception of divine inspiration has gained ground—one that has admittedly been popularised by Christian scholars with a theological axe to grind, but which can be fruitfully adopted by Jews and which is not, if rightly understood, a radical departure from Jewish tradition.

This is the view stated above that in the Bible we have the divine message conveyed to us through the activities and the thoughts of human beings. The Bible in this view is the record of a *dialogue* between God and man; it can be compared, to use Robertson Smith's illustration, to the report of a conversation between a father and his child in which not only the sagacious contribution of the father is given but the baby-talk of the child, without which the report would be incomplete. This means that in the Bible we have the record of man searching for God and God disclosing Himself to man and the corollary to this, that, at times, man's vision of the truth as recorded in the Bible, is imperfect. This view, though unconventional, is not very far removed from the full implications of the rabbinic teaching that the Torah speaks in the language of men. It is in line with the view of Maimonides that just as God did not lead His people in their physical Exodus the 'way of the land of the Philistines' because 'it was near' so too in their spiritual pilgrimage their divine Teacher preferred to wean them *gradually* away from baser notions of religion, allowing His truth slowly to unfold itself to them just as the sound pedagogue encourages his pupils to work out the truth for themselves.[1]

According to this way of looking at the Bible, it is possible to recognise in it higher and lower stages of spiritual development. The eternal truths expressed in such verses as 'Thou shalt love thy neighbour as thyself',[2] 'In the beginning God created the heavens and the earth',[3] 'So God created man in His image',[4] are in no way invalidated because they are to be found in a book which reflects the thought-patterns and uses the language of the times in which it was compiled. The Bible is thus seen to be eternal truth expressing itself in the framework of time. As has been said, a thing is not true because it is in the Bible, it is in the Bible because it is true.

---

[1] Guide, Part III, Chapter 32.
[2] Lev. xix. 18.
[3] Gen. i. 1.
[4] Gen. i. 27.

But, it will be asked, if there are higher and lower teachings in the Bible how are we to recognise which are higher and which lower, how are we to distinguish between the eternal and the ephemeral? The answer is, surely, that the distinction is perceived by the human heart and worked out in Jewish tradition. We accept command such as 'Love thy neighbour as thyself' as true for all time because we instinctively realise that its appeal is to our higher nature, we discover a response to its challenge, an echo to its call, in the depths of our own soul. And Jewish tradition, the *Torah She-Be-'Al Peh*, the Oral Torah, what Schechter called 'the Secondary Meaning of the Bible', the sum-total of Jewish research into the Bible and Jewish application of its teachings throughout the ages, this has always given expression to the *eternal* values while avoiding the application of those which have had their day.

The story is told of a Catholic Cardinal who had to share a taxi with a Protestant Archbishop. 'After all', said the Cardinal, waving away the Archbishop's protest, 'we both serve the same God. You serve Him in your way, I serve Him in *His*'! But there is a third way between serving God in our own way and in serving Him in what the Cardinal called 'His'. We are not obliged to adopt an outlook of religious anarchy merely because we do not accept an authoritarian view. For, rightly understood, the human effort to discover the will of God is itself part of that will. As the famous Hasidic saint, Levi Yitzchak of Berditchev said, 'the Written Torah contains the divine eternal light, which cannot be endured by itself. The Oral Torah is the human restriction—*Tzimtzum*—of that light so that it can be endured and allowed to illumine human life'. Or, to put this thought in the language of our day, the Word of God must be constantly applied to life, its potentialities realised and its rigours softened, so that men may live by it.

It is this that really matters, that no representative Jewish teacher has ever encouraged his followers to engage in religious persecution in obedience to the texts which speak of the destruction of the Canaanites, while many Jewish teachers developed and applied those texts which express the brotherhood of man to yield such universalistic, practical teachings as that the devout Jew is obliged to support the poor, clothe the naked, heal the sick and comfort the mourners of the Gentile peoples in the same way as he is duty bound to carry out these obligations to his own people.

This is why such a statement as the following by a twentieth century historian, leaves Jews unmoved: 'Besides the logic of its doctrines, the character of its Sacred Book must also be held partly accountable for the intolerant principles of the Christian Church. It was unfortunate that the early Christians had included in their Scripture the Jewish writings which reflect the ideas of a low stage of civilisation and are full of savagery. It would be difficult to say how much harm has been done, in corrupting the morals of men, by the precepts and examples of inhumanity, violence and bigotry which the reverent reader of the Old Testament, implicity believing in its inspiration, is bound to approve. It furnished an armoury for the theory of persecution. The truth is that the Sacred Books are an obstacle to moral and religious progress, because they consecrate the ideas of a given epoch, and its customs, as divinely appointed. Christianity, by adopting books of a long past age, placed in the path of human development a particularly nasty stumbling block.'[1] For it is precisely this 'consecration of a given epoch and its customs as divinely appointed' against which the doctrine of the Oral Torah guards. The Rabbis frequently describe a Biblical practice which they held could no longer be applied, as *horaath shaah*, 'a temporary measure', lit. a 'teaching for the hour'. Nowhere is the differing attitudes of Synagogue and Church in this matter seen more clearly than on the question of the persecution of witches. How many unfortunate women were judicially murdered in Europe in obedience to the literal interpretation and application of the verse: 'Thou shalt not suffer a witch to live'?[2] In the Synagogue, on the other hand, the verse never received literal fulfilment. The ancient Rabbis developed a whole system of restrictions which made capital punishment a virtual impossibility, in spite of the fact that it is sanctioned in the Bible. (Even if I. H. Weiss and others are correct in suggesting that these restrictions were purely

[1] J. B. Bury: *A History of Freedom of Thought*, Oxford University Press 1952, p. 38.
[2] Exodus xxii. 17.

academic and theoretical the tendency is beyond dispute. Akiba and Tarfon did say: 'Had we have been in the Sanhedrin none would ever have been put to death'.[1] And with the establishment of the State of Israel, the *Keneseth* abolished capital punishment as a logical development of the traditional attitude). Similarly, no Jewish teacher has objected to the use of anæsthetics in childbirth, as a prominent Christian divine is said to have done, on the basis of the curse in Genesis[2] that travail should be in pain.[3]

Applying the pragmatic test, and it is this that counts, Judaism has not been guilty of religious intolerance. Judaism does not know of Inquisitions, of Crusades, of Holy Wars. The fact that Jews have rarely had the opportunity of engaging in these does not substantially affect the argument, for this in itself has been a powerful contributory factor to a more tolerant interpretation of religious zeal in Judaism. In the words of the Midrash, the burning bush seen by Moses at the beginning of his ministry, though burning with fire, was not consumed and did not consume the surrounding bushes. The divine fire burned brightly in the Jewish soul without destroying itself by seeking to destroy those in whose soul there existed not a spark of that fire. For the evidence of history and our deepest convictions are at one in teaching that it is suicidal for a religion to seek to perpetuate itself by persecution, that the book is a mightier weapon than the sword, and that the bush which does not consume will not itself be consumed.

[1] Makk. i. 10.
[2] Gen. iii. 16.
[3] Cf. H. J. Zimmels: *Magicians, Theologians and Doctors*, Lond., 1952, p. 6.

CHAPTER IX

The Study and Practice of the Torah

IF the Torah is the Will of God then its study must be a
religious duty. And, indeed, Judaism elevates the study of
the Torah as the supreme religious duty. When a Talmudic
Rabbi took an unduly long time over his prayers, his friends
rebuked him: 'They neglect eternal life (the study of the
Torah) and engage in temporal existence' (the habit of
prayer).[1] And such study, it was taught, was meritorious not
alone because of its practical application, not alone because
without it the Israelite would not know what to *do*, but because
the theoretical contemplation of God's will as revealed in the
Torah was considered to be in itself the highest of religious
aims. Study was a means of worship, of 'thinking God's
thoughts after Him' and so linking the human mind with the
divine. Hence the intensive cultivation of Jewish learning as a
noble end in itself, absorbing generations of brilliant minds
even in those fields which could have no practical bearing on
Jewish life, such as the regulations concerning the Temple
service and the complex sacrificial system.

When the Talmudist tried to master the treatise which
deals with laws such as that of the ox goring the cow and
hoped to add his mite to the wealth of ingenious commentary and super-commentary, he knew that it was exceedingly
improbable that at any stage in his career he would be called
upon to render actual legal decisions on these questions. But
he was convinced that the divine wisdom is expressed in every
one of the Torah laws, irrespective of its frequency or practic-
ability. Whether his subject was the laws of fraud and breach
of contract or the rules governing prayer and worship, he
believed himself to be in contact with the spirit of the Torah,
and this not only because Judaism enjoins the sanctification of
day-to-day pursuits but because whatever one studied the

[1] Sabb. 10a.

93

attempt of grasping God's will was being made. The detailed laws were, in fact, looked upon as concrete illustration of abstract Torah principles. The learned Talmudist would have been as little moved by the scorn poured on him for considering abstruse legal cases which could never happen as the pure mathematician for debating how long it would take three men working at different speeds to empty a pond.

Of all the spiritual types produced by Jews, none has had a longer and more continuous tradition than the *Talmid Hakham*, as the student of Torah was called. The *Talmid Hakham* of today may be different in many respects from his counterparts of the Talmudic period and the Middle Ages, yet he sees himself, with justice, as their spiritual heir in that he devotes his life, as they did theirs, to the ideal of Torah study by complete submission to its rigorous discipline.

We have no clear evidence as to when the term *Talmid Hakham*—disciple of the wise—was first used. The suggestion that Jewish sages, in their humility, have always spoken of themselves as 'disciples' is homiletically inspiring no doubt, but historically unsound. The facts are that the term is not met with before the second Century C.E. Before that time scholars were spoken of as *Hakhamim*—Sages. In Ethics of the Fathers, for instance, we read that Jose, the son of Joezer, of Zeredah, who flourished about 170 B.C.E., said: 'Let thy house be a meeting place for *Hakhamim*'[1]—not for *Talmide Hakhamim*.

The authoritative definition of the epithet *Talmid Hakham* is found in the following passage: 'If one says to a woman: "Behold thou are consecrated to me (in marriage) on the understanding that I am a *Talmid Hakham*", it is not necessary for him to be as diligent a student as Simeon ben Azzai or Simeon ben Zoma (c. 130 C.E.). The marriage is valid if he is sufficiently well-versed in his studies to be able to give an answer to any question put to him in them, even if he is studying the (small) tractate *Kallah*. If he says: "On the understanding that I am a Sage" (*Hakham*), it is not necessary for him to be like the Sages of Jabneh, like R. Akiba (flourished c. 110–135 C.E.) and his contemporaries. The marriage is valid if he can answer any question put to him on general matters of wisdom (i.e. not

[1] Aboth. i. 4.

in any *one* subject)[1] Here a distinction is drawn between the *Hakham*—the sage—described as the scholar proficient in general learning, and the *Talmid Hakham*, the man proficient in his immediate studies only. On the other hand, in his famous homily on the verse: 'Thou shalt fear the Lord thy God',[2] R. Akiba remarks that this includes the reverence due to the *Talmid Hakham*,[3] and the reverence is clearly to the mature scholar. In the later literature the term is used exclusively of the mature scholar.

It appears that, at first, the term used for the sage was *hakham*. Then there was a transition period in which both terms were used, one for the sage, the other for his disciples. And, finally, the term *hakham* fell into disuse and the term *talmid hakham* alone was used of every type of scholar. It may well have been that as a result of Roman attempts at abolishing ordination, the older term was replaced by one suggesting inferior status so as to avoid awakening the suspicions of the oppressors. All we can say with certainty, however, is that by the third century the accepted term for the scholar was *talmid hakham*, or its Aramaic equivalent, *zurba merabbanan*.

What was the nature of the intellectual activity in which the *Talmid Hakham* engaged? A brief answer would be, the study and interpretation of the Torah. No doubt, some of the Talmudic sages were familiar with Greek culture and the Greek language, with Roman institutions, with the scientific knowledge of their day. Certainly, many mediaeval scholars were philosophers, grammarians, poets, astronomers and physicians, but such pursuits were extensions of *halachic* (Jewish legal) studies, by virtue of which alone they acquired the right to be called *Talmide Hakhamim*. When the famous Jewish moralist of the last century, R. Israel Salanter, was asked: 'Why is it that in former times the Rabbis were physicians and men of broad general culture whereas nowadays they confine their studies to the 'four ells of the Halachah'? he replied: 'Why is it that in former ages the physicians and men of broad general culture were Rabbis, whereas nowadays they are ignorant of Jewish learning'?

The *Talmid Hakham* considered his chief task to be that of

[1] Tos. Kidd. III. 10, Kidd. 49b.   [2] Deut. vi. 13.   [3] B.K. 41b.

interpreter of the traditions. He was no innovator. It is no coincidence that Jesus' Jewish contemporaries were shocked at his advancement of the claim to teach as an 'original thinker' in religious matters. 'It hath been said . . . But *I say* unto you . . .'[1]

Yet it would be a mistake to assume that the *Talmid Hakham* looked upon his rôle as that of a mere mechanical transmitter and expounder of long-established truths. There was not lacking the idea that his function included a certain creativity in Torah life and thought. Thus, we find *Talmide Hakhamim* in all ages introducing enactments of various kinds with the purpose of making the Torah law applicable to changing conditions. Among the more well-known of these are the ban on polygamy by the Synod of Gershom of Mayence (c. 1,000 C.E.); the same Synod's outlawing of divorce without the wife's consent; Hillel's *prosbol;* the institution of the *Kethubah* (marriage settlement) to protect the interests of the wife; the many 'fences' built round the Torah for its protection; and, in the field of ritual, the introduction of new observances such as the washing of the hands before meals and the kindling of the Hannukah lights. We have noted that the benediction to be recited before the performance of these latter duties is: 'Who hath sanctified us with His commandments and commanded us . . .': the right of the *Talmid Hakham* to introduce such innovations was considered to be of divine origin. In the realm of pure academic learning there was likewise much scope for originality. The sanction for the discovery of new truths within the old resulted in much original activity, as is evidenced by the numerous volumes of *novellae* on the Talmudic literature.

A prominent feature of the intellectual life of the *Talmud Hakham* was the assiduity with which he applied himself to his studies. Completely absorbed in his learning, his mind filled with halachic problems and their solutions, with subtle distinctions and fine points of law, with arguments in favour of the schools he followed and devastating criticisms of those he opposed, he had little or no inclination for the more mundane of life's pleasures. Not that he was a conscious ascetic. Bertrand

[1] But some scholars think that Jesus was, in fact, using here the usual method of Bible interpretation found frequently in the Rabbinic literature, see David Daube's *The New Testament and Rabbinic Judaism*, Lond., 1956, pp. 55–62.

Russell's description of the philosopher can serve just as well for the *Talmid Hakham*. 'The philosopher will not abstain with an effort from the pleasures of sense, but will be thinking of other things. I have known many philosophers who forgot their meals, and read a book when at last they did eat. These men were acting as Plato said they should: they were not abstaining from gluttony by means of a moral effort, but were more interested in other matters. Apparently the philosopher should marry, and beget and rear children, in the same absent-minded way, but since the emancipation of women this has become more difficult. No wonder Xanthippe was a shrew'. It is recorded that Rabbi Joseph Rosen, the world-renowned Gaon of Ragadshov, grew his hair long rather than waste at the barber's a precious half-hour that could be devoted to Torah study, and that on his wedding day he had to be reminded of the time of the ceremony so engrossed was he in his studies. In Talmudic times, the *Talmid Hakham* was advised when choosing a wife to take with him an ignorant man to see the lady[1]—the Rabbis evidently believing that a man's capacity for assessing feminine charm decreases in inverse ratio to his prowess in learning. In view of this assiduity we need not be surprised at the regulation forbidding a *Talmid Hakham* to enter an alley into which refuse had been deposited, for it is not seemly to have the mind on the Torah in such surroundings, and for a *Talmid Hakham* to remain for any length of time without thinking on the Torah is an impossibility![2]

This devotion to study manifested itself especially in the Middle Ages, when it was not unusual for the students of the French Academies to spend all their week-days and nights in the house of learning, snatching a few hours sleep at their benches. In our own day, many of the students in the Yeshiboth of Lithuania and Poland would study for as many as sixteen hours a day. Naturally, such devotion resulted in an unparalleled familiarity with the sources. I have known *Talmide Hakhamim* of the old school who knew practically the whole of the Babylonian Talmud—a work containing about 2,500,000 words —by heart.

As a result of his absorption in study and the influence of the

---

[1] B.B. 168a.   [2] Ber. 24b.

Torah on his life, even the small talk of the *Talmid Hakham* acquired, as it were, a Torah flavour. The Rabbinic saying to this effect was thus paraphrased by Boswell, in the name of the prelate Secker, as his justification for recording the small talk of Dr. Johnson. 'Even the idle words of a good man ought to be recorded, the most superfluous things he saith are of some value'.

There is much material in the Rabbinic sources on the character of the *Talmid Hakham*, but before quoting some of this material a word of warning must be sounded. Every student of the Talmud knows how difficult it is, especially when dealing with Aggadic material, to know how far a statement expressing values is a reflection of actual conditions or an idealised picture seldom realised in actual life. Many of the demands made on the *Talmid Hakham* in this literature are far too severe for all, or even most of them, to have been realised in the person of the average *Talmid Hakham*. In fact fierce denunciations of the faults to which *Talmide Hakhamim* are prone show that scholars possessed their quota of human failings. If, for instance, we find great teachers constantly urging *Talmide Hakhamim* to endeavour to eradicate pride from their lives, we are justified in concluding that the lesson was needed.

A *Talmid Hakham*, the Talmud tells us, was required to be cleanly and neatly dressed: if a stain were found on his garments, it was hyperbolically observed, he was deserving of death.[1] Yet too great an extravagance in dress was frowned upon. When a Palestinian scholar was asked why the Babylonians resemble the ministering angels in the splendour of their dress, he ironically replied that such ostentation is an attempt at compensation for their deficiencies in learning.[2] As a further means of upholding the dignity of his station, the *Talmid Hakham* was advised against partaking of meals indiscriminately outside his own home.[3] But with typical rabbinic regard for the dignity of self-supporting labour, he was advised to perform even the most menial tasks in order to earn his living.[4]

It was naturally expected of the *Talmid Hakham* that he be scrupulous in his religious observances and ethical conduct. 'He

[1] Sabb. 114a.   [3] Pes. 49a.
[2] Sabb. 145b.   [4] Pes. 113a.

who says: 'I will have nothing but Torah' (i.e. he will give no thought to practice but to study alone) has not even Torah to his credit'[1] is a typical saying. Similarly, the Shulchan Aruch, the standard Code of Jewish law, rules that a *Talmid Hakham* who is lax in his religious observance has no greater claim to respect than the meanest member of the community.[2] On the other hand it was recognised that genius is a law unto itself with its own peculiar temptations. 'The greater the man, the greater his evil inclination' observed one teacher.[3] Another teacher remarked that it is the fire of the Torah burning in his soul which causes an irascible *Talmid Hakham* to act in a high-handed manner.[4] Indeed, some degree of severity was expected of the *Talmid Hakham*, which explains such statements as that a *Talmid Hakham* who does not take revenge like a snake or who is not as hard as iron is no *Talmid Hakham*.[5] But on the whole the reputation of *Talmide Hakhamim* was so good that it could be said: 'If thou seest a *Talmid Hakham* commit a sin by night, entertain no condemnatory thought about him next day, for he has certainly repented'.[6]

What was the relationship between the *Talmid Hakham* and the people he was called upon to lead? In early Talmudic times no love was lost between the *Talmid Hakham* and the *'Am Ha'aretz* (lit. 'people of the land'), as the man ignorant of Torah was called. Such sayings as: 'It is permitted to kill an *'Am Ha'aretz* even on Yom Kippur which falls on the Sabbath'[7] have, of course, to be taken with more than a grain of salt, but they are indicative of the deep-seated hatred between the two classes. The ignorant on their side were not inarticulate. The great R. Akiba said that when he was an *'Am Ha'aretz* he said: 'Who will deliver a *Talmid Hakham* into my hands that I might bite him as an ass bites'.[8] But on the whole the community took pride in its scholars and acquiesced in the granting of special privileges to them. Concessions were granted to scholars in their business dealings to enable them to earn their living with ease and thus have more time for study. Pedlars of trinkets were not allowed to set up stalls in the towns they visited but were

1 Yeb. 109b.   5 Yom. 23a, Ta'an. 4a.
2 Y.D. 243.3.   6 Ber. 19a.
3 Sukk. 52b.   7 Pes. 49b.
4 Ta'an. 4a.   8 Pes. *ibid.*

allowed only to sell their wares at the house doors. A scholar-pedlar was, however, allowed to set up a stall.[1] It is told of R. Dimi of Nehardea that he came to the town of Mahoza to sell some dried figs, whereupon the Exilarch instructed Raba (d. 357 C.E.) to give him a test in learning and, if he demonstrated his proficiency, a proclamation should be issued that no other dealer be allowed to sell figs until R. Dimi had sold his.[2] From the incidental manner in which the Talmud refers to this it would seem that it was quite usual for proclamations of this kind to have been issued in favour of visiting scholars. A further concession of much importance was the exemption of scholars from taxation. The Jewish Community paid the scholar's share to the Government from the Community Chest.[3] Butchers were obliged to sell the choicest portions of their meat to the scholars or their retainers, who were allowed to buy before all other customers.[4]

So concerned were the Talmudic teachers to uphold the dignity of the *Talmid Hakham* that they allowed him to place those who had offended him under a ban.[5] A man who insulted a *Talmid Hakham* was obliged to pay him a 'pound of gold'.[6] (These privileges were, at times, abused so that in the later Rabbinic literature we find the suggestion made, and eventually adopted, that for the purpose of the ban and for the 'pound of gold' there are no *Talmide Hakhamim* nowadays.)[7] It is well known that the Rabbis interpreted the Biblical command to rise before the aged,[8] to refer also to the Talmid Hakham.[9]

It cannot be too strongly emphasized that the major intellectual pursuit of the *Talmid Hakham* through the ages was *halachic* study. With one or two notable exceptions, works in English on Rabbinic thought concentrate almost entirely on *Aggadic*[10] material, with the kind of distortion that would result if writers on Shakespeare persisted in judging his work by the

---

[1] B.B. 22a.
[2] B.B. *ibid.*
[3] B.B. 8a, Ned. 62b.
[4] Kidd. 70a.
[5] M.K. 16a.
[6] Yer. B.K. 8.6.
[7] Y.D. 243.7,8.
[8] Lev. xix. 32.
[9] Kidd. 32b.

[10] Halachah = the legal side of Judaism, the rules and regulations of Jewish Law and the expositions on which they are based. Aggadah = all the non-legal material in the Jewish sources, i.e. the ethics, philosophy, history, folk-lore and popular sayings of the Jews.

sonnets with barely a hint that he wrote plays. There is a real lack of good biographical material of the great *halachists* and on the way in which their lives were governed by the *halachic* approach. One of the few works worth reading in this field is the recently published volume of studies by S. Sevin[1] on the great Lithuanian giants of the *halachah* in the nineteeth and twentieth centuries.

So far we have noted the rôle of the *Talmid Hakham* in the traditional scheme of Jewish life. No apology is offered for space given to this theme in a work on Jewish theology, for the ideal of the *Talmid Hakham* belongs to the glorious spiritual achievements of Judaism. But one of the most acute problems for religious Jews today is whether the *Talmid Hakham* still has a place in the modern Jewish setting. With the advent of the Emancipation, Jewish talent has been directed into other channels than that of pure Jewish learning. Even the Rabbi has, nowadays, so many subjects to master, from modern psychology and philosophy to general literature and history, that even if he is Orthodox, he is generally far more a pastor, an administrator, a social worker, a preacher, a philosopher, or a theologian, than a *Talmid Hakham*. And it is not alone that today 'secular' studies have their legitimate claim on the scholar's time and interest. The study of the Jewish sources themselves has been revolutionised by the new critical methods of the historical school. Although these methods do not in themselves give rise to the suggestion that the ideal of the *Talmid Hakham* can no longer be of service, there is the tacit assumption among many scholars that *Jüdische Wissenschaft* (as the scientific study of Jewish sources has been called) has completely superseded the older learning for which the *Talmid Hakham* was renowned. The term 'Jewish scholar' carries with it today generally the meaning of one who avails himself of 'scientific' methods of investigation, in which nothing is taken for granted without evidence, in which long established traditions are critically examined and in which the sociological, political and historical forces governing the emergence and development of Jewish institutions are uncovered and brought to light. And, as we have noted in the previous chapters, this activity does not

[1] *'Ishim We-Shittoth*, Jer. 1952.

cease, and these methods are still employed, even when the most sacred texts are studied. Obviously, against such a background it is not easy to preserve that attitude of mind which enabled the *Talmid Hakham* to delve patiently and serenely into the Bible and Talmud confident that he was discovering the will of God.

But there are growing signs of recognition on the part of members of both the critical and traditional schools that it is possible and advantageous to combine the old and new learning so as to bring to Jewish studies both the accuracy and objectively of the critical scholar and the devotional spirit, befitting researches into sacred literature, of the *Talmid Hakham*. Once it is recognised that 'the seal of the Holy One, blessed is He, is Truth', there is no reason for either a lukewarm attitude (devoid of reverence and enthusiasm for Jewish traditional and religious values) on the part of critical students of the Jewish sources, or a lack of objectivity on the part of *Talmide Hakhamim*.

The old gibe has it that the *Talmid Hakham* knows what Abaye said, while the Professor of Semitics only knows what kind of trousers he wore. The truth of the matter is that Jewish scholars nowadays are becoming increasingly aware that the *Talmid Hakham* would be better equipped to understand what Abaye really said if he were familiar with the kind of subject taught at modern rabbinical seminaries and in the Semitics Departments at Universities. And the Professor can no longer be content, if he is to understand the true spirit of Judaism, with historical and philological investigation alone. And this applies not only to Rabbis and Professors. The layman too can recapture, if he is so minded, the grand old Jewish ideal of the study of the Torah for its own sake. This study will be carried out in a spirit of devotion, it will still be a religious duty of the highest order even though it will include the researches made by critical scholars many of whom were not Jews or not religious Jews. He will in fact not be content to search *into* the Torah but to search *for* the Torah, to use every tried method of investigation as God-given. For he will know that the search for the Torah is itself Torah and that to use Bahya Ibn Pakudah's famous illustration, there can be no act more pleasing to the king than the attempt of his subject to read and understand the letter the king has sent to him.

No serious student today can afford to neglect the historical approach to Jewish studies. But the mistake so often made is to assume that if as a result of this approach, an idea is placed in its proper historical perspective, it has no longer any value for us today. Whereas the religious mind will not be content with historical explanation but will seek to discover the permanent values of the tradition and to seek in them guidance and inspiration for the present. As C. S. Lewis so skilfully makes his 'tempter' say in the Screwtape Letters: 'Only the learned read old books and we (the devils) have now so dealt with the learned that they are of all men the least likely to acquire wisdom by doing so. We have done this by inculcating the Historical Point of View'.

If this is true of 'secular' studies how much more true is it of Torah study where the divine is constantly seeking to express itself through the human and is ready to break in on the student with flashes of spiritual illumination so that his whole outlook is transformed. 'Remember the days of old, consider the years of many generations; ask thy father and he will shew thee; thy elders and they will tell thee'.[1]

So far we have spoken of the problems of Jewish study. But the far more practical problem for Jews today is that of Jewish observance. How can we go on submitting to the rigorous demands of traditional Judaism, many ask, if the critical view as to some of its origins are accepted? Do not these views shatter our confidence in the divine nature of some of the Jewish observances? The answer, according to the view of Torah sketched above, is that knowledge of the lowly origin of certain Jewish practices, need not cause us to lose faith, for it is not the origin of a religious practice that matters, but what it has become, the highest form in which it has been expressed. And this is in itself the will of God. No one argues, to give an example from another field, that because modern medicine grew out of magic it has no value, or that the beauty and value of a Rembrandt is in any way affected by the incontrovertible fact that Art began in the caves of the Stone Age.

[1] Deut. xxxii. 7.

To make this point clear one or two examples must be given. Supposing a Jew reads and examines closely all that has been written on the question of the origin of *Tefillin* and *Mezuzah*, and his reading convinces him that the original meaning of 'And thou shalt bind them for a sign upon thine hand, and they shall be as frontlets between thine eyes. And thou shalt write them upon the posts of thy house, and on thy gates'[1] had no reference to these observances but was a figurative way of saying that the word of God should be before the Israelite at all times.[2] But seeing that from the very earliest times these words were interpreted to mean that the Jew should don the *Tefillin* and affix the *Mezuzah* to the doors of his house, these observances are now part of the Torah, part of the totality of Jewish religious expression, concrete ways of recalling the principles expressed in these verses.

Or take the festivals of Purim and Hannukah. If as a result of his studies into the origins of these festivals, a Jew is convinced that the eight days of Hannukah were not introduced, as the Talmudic legend has it, in commemoration of the miracle of the oil, but to correspond to the eight days of Tabernacles,[3] or he doubts the historicity of the events recorded in the book of Esther, this will not prevent him from observing these festivals in the traditional way. For he will know that the message of Esther that God protects His people and that tyranny does not triumph, and the message of the oil that spiritual light, though small at first, increases in splendour, are of the utmost value in furthering the spiritual life of the Jewish people.

This approach has found many distinguished exponents in modern times—prominent among them, Zecharias Frankel, Solomon Schechter and, in our day, Louis Ginzberg. Basically, it is the old idea, permeating the whole of the traditional literature, that rabbinic laws and enactments are binding on Jews because—though, of course, it is not put in this way in the older sources—they are part of that interaction between the divine and the human that is Torah. If the Torah is the result

---

[1] Deut. vi. 8–9.
[2] But see above p. 40f.
[3] See II Macc. i. 9; x. 6, and J. E. Vol. VI, p. 223f.

of both God's unfolding will and man's attempt to discover and apply that will then all the spiritual riches of Judaism are Torah and justifiably claim our allegiance.

There is a discussion in the Midrash on the verse: 'The Torah of the Lord is perfect, restoring the soul'.[1] One Rabbi says that the meaning is that because the Torah of the Lord is perfect, *therefore* it restores the soul. The other Rabbi interprets the verse to mean, *because* it restores the soul, therefore it is perfect.[2] It is not suggested that the Rabbis of the Midrash could have anticipated our problem, but here you have in a nutshell the difference in approach between the mediaeval and the modern approach to Jewish observance. The mediaeval approach was the heteronomous one. Jews in the Middle Ages rarely spoke of the 'beauties' of the Jewish way of life. The contemplation of God's perfect will, as revealed in the Torah, filled them with awe. It was sufficient for them that they obey unquestioningly and without hesitation, and no student of the Middle Ages can fail to recognise the spiritual grandeur of their lives. Nowadays we know far more than they did about Jewish origins. We are inclined to recognise the *human* element in the Torah to a far greater extent than they could have done. But we too accept the Torah as the word of God because we can witness the *effects* of Jewish observance. Those very historical studies we thought might undermine our confidence in the Torah have, in fact, strengthened it, for they have enabled us to appreciate it for the vital, dynamic principle that it is. We can observe how the traditional way of Sabbath observance, the dietary laws, the benedictions and the prayers, the Tzitzith, the Tefillin, the Mezuzah, the Synagogue and its ritual, the festivals and their laws and customs, have all contributed to the ennoblement of Jewish life and the elevation of the Jewish spirit. And these observances, moreover, carried out in the spirit of dedication and inner consecration in which they were intended to be carried out, can do for twentieth century Jews what they succeeded so well in doing for Jews of former ages. Our valid approach is, as Rosenzweig said, 'from the periphery to the centre' so that we say with the Rabbi of old: 'Because the Torah restores the soul therefore it is perfect'!

[1] Psalms XIX. 8.   [2] Yalkut, Teh. 674.

CHAPTER X

Miracles

THERE are two distinct questions to be considered in any discussion of miracles: (*a*) are miracles possible? (*b*) if they are possible did they occur and can they occur now?

A miracle is generally understood to be an event so at variance with the way nature generally behaves that it can only be explained as the result of *super*natural intervention. In everyday parlance the word is frequently used for any unusual or unexpected happening, especially of some religious or moral significance, such as the successful evacuation of the British Troops at Dunkirk or the emergence of the State of Israel, but these events can be explained without invoking the supernatural. Some Jewish sources do speak, indeed, of two kinds of miracle—the *revealed* miracle, where the Hand of God is clearly and incontrovertibly observed, and the *hidden* miracle in which God works, as it were, behind the scenes 'and only he who sees takes off his shoes'. The ten plagues, the parting of the Red Sea, the manna from Heaven, the revival of the dead children by Elijah and Elisha, are examples of the first; the deliverance of the Jews from destruction by the complex series of apparently unrelated events related in the book of Esther, an example of the second.

It is true that even the first kind of miracle has been explained as the result of natural causes—the ten plagues as natural manifestations, the parting of the sea as the effect of a tidal wave, the manna as the fruit of a shrub which grows in the Sinai peninsula, the water from the rock as issuing from a subterranean stream, the episode of the talking ass as occurring in a dream, and the recovery of the children as a revival not from death but from a cataleptic state similar to it—and this by some of the most renowned Jewish commentators. But, on the whole, the view is consistently maintained right through the Rabbinic literature that miracles are possible and that they did occur in both Biblical and Rabbinic times. Furthermore the concept of a divine interruption of nature's laws is behind the many prayers of petition to be found in the Prayer Book. The devout Jew prays for the sick to be healed, for rain to fall, for the crops to grow, not, be it said, as an excuse for human effort, but in the belief, nonetheless, that prayer can prevent (though it may not always do so) the operation of natural causes. He believes, in other words, that God performs miracles.

It should, however, be noted, that while the Prayer Book does contain prayers of petition, in which divine aid is invoked to change the course of nature, these are always requests for God to perform 'hidden' miracles. There are no requests that God should perform a 'revealed' miracle. So too in the thanksgiving prayer, praise is given to God for his 'daily miracles'— 'We will give thanks unto Thee . . . for Thy miracles which are daily with us, and for Thy wonders and Thy benefits which are wrought at all times . . .'[1] The Mishnah in fact states that a prayer for God to alter events, which have already taken place, in the worshipper's favour is a 'vain prayer'. 'If a man cries out to God over what is past, his prayer is vain. Thus if his wife was with child and he said: "May it be Thy will that my wife shall bear a male", this prayer is vain. If he was returning from a journey and heard a sound of lamentation in the city and said: "May it be Thy will that they which make lamentation be not of my house", this prayer is vain.'[2] It is considered presumptuous for a man to ask God so to change the course of natural events on his behalf that he will be *aware* that a miracle has been performed for him, for such a request implies that he alone is worthy of the clear revelation of God's Power denied to other men. Then again if such an evident manifestation of God's Power were shown to a man this would have the effect of depriving him of his freedom of choice, at least so far as faith is concerned, for who could have religious doubts if confronted with such evidence?[3]

[1] Singer's *Prayer Book*, p. 51.
[2] Ber. IX. 3.
[3] For an interesting discussion of this point see Rabbi A. Dessler's: *Mikhtab MeElijahu*, Lond., 1955, p. 177f.

The argument against miracles is sufficiently well-known. There are, it is claimed, inexorable laws which must operate without reference to man's needs or desires—if water is subjected to intense heat it must boil, to intense cold it must freeze; if iron is thrown into water it must sink; if a stone is thrown into the air it must eventually drop and it is inconceivable that it remain suspended in mid-air without human intervention.

Now some of the Rabbis believed that the religious mind ought not to hanker after miracles: that it was a kind of religious Philistinism not to be content to accept the natural order as the will of God and as wonderful in itself, as can be seen from the following Talmudic anecdote. A man's wife died leaving him with a babe for whom he was unable to afford a nurse. A miracle was performed for him and his breasts became as a woman's that he might suckle his child. One of the Rabbis said: 'How great this man must have been that such a miracle was performed for him'. But another Rabbi commented: 'On the contrary! How unworthy this man must have been that the order of creation was changed on his behalf.'[1] There can be no doubt that in this bizarre example we have a widely held rabbinic opinion, reflected in later Jewish literature, that there is religious vulgarity in desiring constant interruptions in the sublime constancy of natural law. Maimonides[2] taught that right at the beginning of creation when natural law was ordained provision was made for miraculous departure from it. Max Kaddushin has shown that this idea is found in two earlier Talmudic passages.

(1) 'Ten things were created on the eve of the first Sabbath of Creation in the twilight: the mouth of the earth,[3] the mouth of the well,[4] the mouth of the ass,[5] the rainbow, the mamma, the rod[6] . . . .'[7]

(2) 'R. Jonathan said: The Holy One, blessed is He, imposed a condition on the sea that it be divided before Israel . . . R. Jeremiah ben Eleazar said: Not on the sea alone did the Holy One, blessed is He, impose such conditions but on all

[1] Sabb. 53b.
[2] *Guide*, II, 29.
[3] Num. xvi. 32.
[4] Num. xxi. 16.
[5] Num. xxii. 28.
[6] Ex. iv. 17.
[7] Aboth v. 6.

that was created in the six days of Creation, as it is said, "I, even My hands, have stretched out the heavens, and all their hosts have I commanded"[1]—I commanded the sea to divide, the fire not to harm Hananiah, Mishael and Azariah, and the lions not to harm Daniel, and the fish to vomit out Jonah'.[2] As Zangwill so effectively expounds this view: 'The Fathers of the Mishnah, who taught that Balaam's ass was created on the eve of Sabbath, in the twilight, were not fantastic fools, but subtle philosophers, discovering the reign of universal law through the exceptions, the miracles that had to be created specially and were still a part of the order of the world, bound to appear in due time much as apparently erratic comets are'.

But with all this 'playing down' of the miraculous there is no *a priori* reason for denying that God *can* perform miracles for doubting that He can change the laws He Himself has ordained. It is important that a distinction be made between the *absolutely* impossible and that which appears impossible to man. The mediæval thinkers used to debate whether God can create a stone which even He cannot pick up. If He cannot create such a stone then He is not omnipotent, for there is something He cannot do. If, on the other hand, He can create such a stone His omnipotence will again be restricted for there will be in existence a stone which He cannot pick up. The fallacy here is a verbal one. If God is omnipotent there cannot *exist* a stone which He cannot pick up. The words 'a stone which God cannot pick up' are meaningless. When we ask: 'Can God create a stone which He cannot pick up' it is as if we asked: 'Can God . . .?' without completing the question. God cannot do the absolutely impossible, i.e. that which is impossible to Him, not because there is any limit to His omnipotence but because there is no such thing. A denial that God can perform a miracle would be valid only if this partook of the nature of the absolutely impossible: but, in fact, the miracle only *appears* impossible to us and is not impossible in any absolute sense.

The real question then is not if miracles *can* happen but if they did, and do, happen. As Hume said long ago, the real

[1] Is. xlv. 12.
[2] B.R. v. 6.

question is one of evidence. It is not adopting a condescending attitude to note that people in 'unscientific' ages were quick to accept as miraculous events that would now be explained as due to the operation of natural laws. An eclipse, for example, as readers of *King Solomon's Mines* will recall, was frequently interpreted as a sign of divine displeasure. In many places drums were beaten at an eclipse to ward off the dragon bent on swallowing the sun or the moon. In addition, hearsay was frequently accepted as evidence in an age when the miraculous did not appear so strange an interruption of nature's laws as it does today. And, as the perusal of the popular press will demonstrate, credulity in such matters was by no means the monopoly of former ages.

The Talmudic Rabbis justly laid it down that a witness in a Jewish Court of Law must not give evidence by hearsay. A famous rabbi was once asked what he thought of the miraculous tales told of their heroes by the followers of the Hasidic wonder-Rabbis. His reply was that he who accepts them is incredibly naïve but he who *cannot* accept them is an unbeliever. This may well be our attitude to the whole question of miracles. To accept uncritically every ancient account of a miracle is to surrender reason, to reject dogmatically every such account is to surrender faith.

In this respect Jews are far less committed to the belief that a *particular* miracle occurred than are Christians whose faith depends on it. This is why the question of miracle does not loom so large in Jewish theology. We have seen that great Jewish commentators had no hesitation in 'rationalising' some of the Biblical miracles. The people of Israel did not believe in Moses because of the miracles he performed, taught Maimonides,[1] but because of the Revelation on Sinai. Saadiah, dealing with this difference between Judaism on the one hand and Christianity and Islam on the other, remarks that our belief in the prophecy of Moses is not due merely to his performance of miracles but to the intrinsic value of his message and that the wonders of a miracle worker would be rejected as proof if he ask us to accept what our reason tells us is wrong. If *A* claims that *B* owes him a large sum of money, the court before

[1] Yad. Yesode Ha-Torah. Chapter VIII.

whom he presents his claim will consider it sympathetically.
But if *A* lays claim to the River Tigris he will be laughed out
of court![1]

One of the strongest arguments against miracles having
occurred is that they do not happen nowadays. Why should
God have chosen to make manifest His Power only in certain
ages? We are admittedly on highly speculative ground here.
But for all we know to the contrary God does perform
miracles for those who trust in Him even today. The Talmud
contains a remarkable discussion of this question.[2] It is said
that miracles were performed on behalf of the third-century
teacher, R. Judah, whereas none were performed on behalf of
later teachers who were more learned in the Law than he.
'When R. Judah drew off his shoes, in times of drought, rain
came immediately but we cry to heaven for days and our
prayers remain unanswered.' The answer given is that the
men of former generations showed a far greater degree of self-
sacrifice in the pursuit of God's truth than we do and miracles
are the fruit of self-sacrifice.[3] Or, as we would put this in the
language of our day, a miracle at any reading of the situation,
is not a kind of divine conjuring trick by means of which God
seeks to impress mortals. It is rather to be understood as the
'natural' result of close human contact with the spiritual
world. The nearer men are to spirituality the stronger its
effects will be manifest in the world of events. Only when the
self is transcended in obedience to the call of the spirit will the
barriers between the natural and the supernatural be broken
down.

Recognising as he must that the doctrine of the deteriora-
tion of the generations has been on the whole a pernicious
one—the loss it produced in initiative is not compensated for
by the gain in humility—and accepting the validity of the
point made above about evidence, the man with an open mind
will not pronounce too readily or dogmatically on the impossibility of the talmudic distinction. It can hardly be denied that

[1] 'Emunoth Ve-Deoth', III, seee Malter's *Saadiah Gaon, His Life and Works*, Phil., 1942, p. 209–210.
[2] Ber. 20a.
[3] Ber. 20a.

in former ages—whatever the faults of those ages from which we are mercifully free—more men lived contemplative lives, and were in closer contact with spiritual things than most men of the hectic twentieth century can be. This is not, of course, to advocate the cultivation of a Chestertonian nostalgia for the 'good old days' but to submit that there may be more things in heaven and earth than are dreamed of in your philosophy. This does not affect the wisdom of the rabbinic teachings concerning the need for people to accept their 'own genera- tion'. Of the Hasidic teacher, R. Simhah Bunem of Pchysca, it is said that he once desired passionately to change places with the patriarch Abraham. How wonderful if I could be Abra- ham and Abraham me? But on deeper reflection he came to the conclusion that this would not do for what would God gain from the substitution? Before the change God would have had among His children an Abraham and a Simhah Bunem and after the change He would still have an Abraham and a Simhah Bunem. And the good Jew ought to desire only that which brings greater glory to God!

CHAPTER XI

The After-Life

THE most striking difference between any modern interpretation of Judaism and the Judaism of Rabbinic and Mediaeval times is the shift in emphasis from an other-wordly to a this-wordly approach to the religious life. Even a cursory inspection of the traditional Jewish classics from the Talmud to Maimonides in the middle ages and to Moses Hayyim Luzzatto (1707-1746) on the threshold of the Emancipation, reveals the persistence of the doctrine of 'Olam Haba (the 'World to Come') in the traditional scheme of Jewish theology.

To deal first with the Talmudic Rabbis, one need not be a particularly erudite rabbinic scholar to observe the strong other-wordly element in rabbinic theology. It is easy to be misled by such sayings as that a man will be obliged to give an account before the Judgment Seat of God for every legitimate pleasure he denies himself,[1] for while it is true that many of the Rabbis were opposed to asceticism (though it must be said that in the wide range of rabbinic religious expression there is room for ascetic tendencies too) this did not prevent them teaching, as, indeed, is implied in this very saying, that this life is a preparation for the After-life. There is no basic incompatibility between the frank acceptance of this world and its pleasures as God-given and the conviction that what a man does with his earthly life is of eternal significance. 'This world is compared to the eve of the Sabbath, the next world to the Sabbath. Only he who toils on the eve of the Sabbath has food to eat on the Sabbath day'.[2] 'This world may be compared to the land and the world to come to the sea. If a man lay not up provisions while on land, what will he eat when at sea'?[3] 'This world is like a vestibule before the world to come. Prepare thyself in the vestibule that thou mayest enter the hall'.[4] These sayings are entirely typical of the rabbinic outlook. Both the

[1] Jer. Kidd. iv. 12.   [2] A.Z. 3a.   [3] Koh. R. to I. 15.   [4] Aboth iv. 16.

Rabbis and Josephus record that the Sadducees rejected the belief in an After-life but the Rabbis, the spiritual heirs of the Pharisees, inherited their beliefs so that such sayings as the above are never contested by any of the Rabbis. All the Rabbis share the belief in the immortality of the soul, it is the background to all they thought and taught. When the *Targum*, the official Aramaic paraphrase of the Bible, interprets the verse: 'Ye shall therefore keep my statutes and my judgments; which if a man do, he shall live in them . . .'[1] to mean 'live in them in life eternal', it was but echoing a commonplace of the rabbinic teaching. One whole chapter of the Talmudic tractate Sanhedrin, deals almost entirely with the subject of the After-life and those who attain it. The Soncino translation in English can be consulted with profit for an account of the fascinating rabbinic views and speculations on *'Olam Haba*.[2] The translator quotes with approval[3] George F. Moore to the effect that although there are many speculations on the After-life in the Talmudic literature 'any attempt to systemise the Jewish notions of the hereafter imposes upon them an order and consistency which does not exist in them'.

During the Middle Ages, belief in the immortality of the soul continued to be held without dissenting voice. Typical of the great mediaeval thinkers is Maimonides, who treats this belief as a cardinal principle of Judaism and speaks disparagingly of those who entertain materialistic conceptions of the Life to Come. 'The good reserved for the righteous is life in the world to come, a life which is immortal, a good without evil. Thus it is written in the Torah: 'That it may be well with thee and that thou mayest prolong thy days';[4] the traditional interpretation of which is as follows: "that it may be well with thee", in a world which is altogether good; "that thou mayest prolong thy days" in a world which is unending, that is, the world to come . . .'

'In the world to come there is nothing corporeal and no material substance; there are only souls of the righteous without bodies, like the ministering angels. And since in that world there are no bodies, there is neither eating nor drinking, nor

[1] Lev. xviii. 5.   [3] P. 601 n. 3.
[2] Pp. 601–765.   [4] Deut. xxii. 7.

aught that human beings need on earth. None of the conditions occur there which are incidental to physical bodies in this world, such as sitting, standing, sleep, death, grief and merriment. So the ancient sages said: "In the life hereafter there is no eating, no drinking, and no marriage, but the righteous sit with their crowns on their heads and enjoy the radiance of the Divine Presence". This passage clearly indicates that as there is no eating or drinking there, there is no physical body hereafter. The phrase "the righteous sit" is allegorical and means that the souls of the righteous exist there without labour or fatigue. The phrase "their crowns on their heads" refers to the knowledge they have acquired and by virtue of which they attained life in the world to come . . . And what is the meaning of the Sages' statement: "they enjoy the radiance of the Divine Presence"? It means that the righteous attain to a knowledge and realisation of the truth concerning God to which they had not attained while they were in the murky and lowly body'.[1]

Moses Hayyim Luzzatto was one of the most colourful personalities in the history of Jewish saintliness. Poet, kabbalist and moralist, he compiled his *Path of the Upright* as a guide to holy living. This work is still studied assiduously by pious Jews striving for self-improvement. The following, from the introduction to the *Path of the Upright*, is indicative of the other-worldly orientation of Luzzatto and his milieu. 'It is fundamentally necessary both for saintliness and for the perfect worship of God to realise clearly what constitutes man's duty in this world, and what goal is worthy of his endeavours throughout all the days of his life.

'Our Sages have taught us that man was created only to find delight in the Lord, and to bask in the radiance of His Presence. But the real place of such happiness is the world to come, which has been created for that very purpose. The present world is a path to that goal. "This world", said our Sages, "is like a vestibule before the world to come". Therefore, has God, blessed be His name, given us the *Mitzvoth*. For this world is the only place where the *Mitzvoth* can be

---

[1] Maimonides, Yad, Hil. Tesh., VIII, see Leon Roth: *The Guide For The Perplexed*, Lond., 1948, p. 114f.

observed. Man is put here in order to earn with the means at his command the place that has been prepared for him in the world to come. In the words of our Sages, "This day is intended for the observance of the *Mitzvoth;* the morrow, for the enjoyment of the reward earned by means of them".[1] No reasonable person can believe that the purpose for which man was created is attainable in this world, for what is man's life in this world? Who is really happy here and who content? "The number of our years is threescore years and ten, or even by reason of strength fourscore years, yet is their pride but travail and vanity",[2] because of the suffering, the sickness, the pain and vexations which man has to endure, and finally death. Hardly one in a thousand finds that the world yields him true pleasure and contentment. And even that one, though he live a hundred years, passes away and is as though he had never been.'

'Moreover, if the purpose for which man was created is attainable in this world, why was he imbued with a soul which belongs to an order of existence higher than that of the angels, especially since the soul cannot enjoy any of the worldly pleasures? In commenting on the verse: "Neither is the soul filled",[3] our Sages add, "The soul may be compared to a princess who is married to a commoner. The most precious gifts that the husband brings to his princess fail to thrill her. Likewise if thou wert to offer the soul all the pleasures of the world, she would remain indifferent to them, because she belongs to a higher order of existence".'[4]

The evidence of these representative quotations—and they could quite easily be multiplied—is conclusive. The mediaeval Jew, like his Christian and Muslim counterpart, looked upon himself as a sojourner here on earth with his real home in heaven. Even in the twentieth century this attitude persisted. It is said that an American millionaire visited the Haphetz Hayyim and was astonished to observe the saint, whose fame had spread all over the Jewish world, living in great frugality. All that his room contained was a bare wooden table and a couple of chairs. 'Where is your furniture, Rabbi?' his guest

---

[1] Err. 22a.   [2] Ps. xc. 10.   [3] Eccl. vi. 7.
[4] Koh. R. to vi. 7., translation of Mordecai M. Kaplan, Philadelphia, 1936.

asked the Haphetz Hayyim. 'And where is your furniture?' the sage asked him. 'My furniture! Why, Rabbi, what do you mean? I am only a visitor. My home is not here'. 'I too am only a visitor and my home is not here'! But in modern Jewish life, and even in modern Jewish religious teaching and preaching, there is an abrupt departure from the whole of the other-worldly conception. Judging by published sermons in English, references to the After-life are not very popular, to say the least, in present-day pulpit oratory.

We need not look far to account for the change. From the time of the French Revolution and the resulting Emancipation of the Jew, the Jewish people faced a problem of adjustment the like of which it had never encountered in its long history. When the walls of the Ghetto fell, Jews had to learn how to live as Jews in Western Society, how to preserve all that was of value in their tradition while participating to the full in the life of those States which had granted them equal civil rights with the rest of the population. Small wonder then that Jewish religious thinkers should have been preoccupied with such matters as Faith and Reason, Universalism and Particularism, Orthodoxy and Reform; all of them problems with immediate bearing on their practical life. The fate and prospects of the Jew in the realm of Eternity was naturally enough overlooked in the urgent struggle to enable Jews to live as good Jews in the world of Time. And no sooner had the bubble of Emancipation been rudely pricked than the beckoning dream of national revival came to the fore. Once again the best of Jewish thinkers busied themselves with immediate concrete problems. Ahad Ha'am and Bialik preached the doctrine of the immortal soul of the people of Israel, urging Jews to make this the object of their striving. In an atmosphere in which the individual Jew who is at all idealistic works for the future of his people, he tends to forget, or, at least, to minimise, the importance of his own personal survival in a future existence.

Side by side with this Jews shared the general decline in belief in the hereafter typical of the past hundred years. The revolt against nineteenth century indifference to shocking social conditions here on earth because of the promise of future bliss, the widening horizons of Science, demonstrating for the first time the impossibility of a Heaven literally above us and a Hell gaping beneath our feet, the Religion versus Science controversy, materialist philosophy, all contributed to the rejection of belief in an After-life. Tennyson's tentative longings in his 'In Memoriam'; the amazing popularity of Fitzgerald's Omar Khayyam; Marx and Lenin castigating religion as the 'opium of the people'; Shaw ridiculing a harp-playing Heaven and a coal-cellar Hell; these are all typical of Victorian and pre-1914 scepticism.

Among non-Jewish religious thinkers, this century has witnessed a reaction in favour of the other-worldly approach. The Great War and its aftermath of suffering, the horrors of Nazism and the concentration camps, the second Global War, the Atom Bomb and the threat of total annihilation have rudely shattered the facile belief that mankind will automatically progress to ever greater heights. No one can shirk today the issues raised by the revelation of man's depravity. So that Christian thinkers in particular are bent on reaffirming the importance of the belief in Immortality for a satisfactory religious outlook. Judaism alone, faced with the many problems raised by the emergence of the State of Israel and given new strength by its exhilarating potentialities, is unlikely to be affected by this reaction in the immediate future. Until the State of Israel is firmly established both materially and spiritually, Jewish thinkers are bound to be pre-eminently concerned with this life and its problems. And who can deny that there is something sublime in the persistent refusal of Jews to turn their back on life, to refuse to give up the struggle to establish the Kingdom of Heaven on earth? But sooner or later, the doctrine of the After-life, so inextricably woven into the fabric of Judaism, must come into its own. No really spiritual interpretation of Judaism is possible without it. The Hamlet of Judaism, if it is to be staged effectively, must not alone include the princely hero, the ghost too must not be omitted.

Is the belief in an After-life a worthy one? It has often been held suspect as pandering to our grasping instincts. It is suggested that it is ignoble for a man who does good to desire reward for so doing, that the whole notion is nothing more

than an attempt at storing up good deeds in a spiritual bank
upon which the calculatingly virtuous may draw. The
believer, so the argument runs, denies himself certain immediate pleasures in the anticipation of more intense delights later
on, much as a man may give up smoking for a time in order
to save up to buy a car or a television set. But the delights of
Heaven as interpreted by Judaism's greatest sons (we have
noted above the views of Maimonides) are *spiritual*. C. S.
Lewis has well said: 'Again, we are afraid that heaven is a
bribe, and that if we make it our goal we shall no longer be
disinterested. It is not so. Heaven offers nothing that a mercenary soul can desire. It is safe to tell the pure in heart that
they shall see God, for only the pure in heart want to. There
are rewards that do not sully motives. A man's love for a
woman is not mercenary because he wants to marry her, nor
his love for poetry mercenary because he wants to read it, nor
his love of exercise less disinterested because he wants to run
and leap and walk. Love, by definition, seeks to enjoy its
object'.[1] And it must not be forgotten that the person who
believes in the After-life generally desires it not for himself
alone but for others too. If it is virtuous to want human happiness to be increased here on earth why should it be considered
ignoble to desire an increase of eternal happiness? Furthermore, without dwelling overmuch on theological niceties, if
God created man for man's good—and this is the only reasonable conclusion to be drawn from belief in a benevolent,
omniscient Creator Who can have lacked nothing before
man's creation—then man, if he does not find complete happiness and fulfilment here on earth must find it in Heaven. Part
of the saintly man's yearning for eternal life is a longing for
God's justice to be vindicated.

In spite of what has been said, Judaism could teach a higher
form of worship from which all thought of personal gain—
even spiritual gain—is absent. 'Be not like servants who
minister to their master upon the condition of receiving a
reward; but be like servants who minister to their master
without the condition of receiving a reward',[2] is the saying of

[1] *The Problem of Pain*, Lond., 1940, p. 133.
[2] Aboth 1. 3.

one of the earliest teachers of the Mishnah. An ancient version of this saying reads 'but be like servants who minister to their master on the *condition of not receiving a reward*' ('*al menath shelo* instead of *shelo 'al menath*).[1] The Hasidic teacher, Schneor Zalman of Ladi, was once overheard saying to himself: 'I desire not Thy Paradise, I desire not Thy Eden, but Thee alone'.

The bitterest complaint against the doctrine of the hereafter is that by directing men's minds heavenwards it diverts them from contemplating social evils and encourages them to tolerate bad social conditions. By it the rich are made complacent and the poor acquiescent. It is not within our purview to consider how far this accusation is justified with regard to other faiths but it is certainly not true of any widely held version of Judaism. In the Hebrew Scriptures the emphasis is so much on justice and righteousness in human affairs here on earth that, as we have been, the Sadducees could accept the Bible as the word of God and yet reject the belief in the hereafter.[2] The idea that the poor can be safely neglected because God will compensate them for their sufferings in the hereafter has always been repugnant to the healthy Jewish religious conscience. Permeated as it is with the doctrine of the Afterlife, the Talmud meticulously surveys the social obligations of the Jew. The Talmudic regulations about such things as Communal taxation, poor relief, care for the sick and infirm, and education of the young show that the Rabbis were possessed of a social conscience far in advance of their time.[3]

It would be futile to speculate on the nature of the Afterlife; Maimonides rightly says that when we discuss this subject we are like blind men trying to understand the nature of light. 'Know that just as a blind man can form no idea of colours nor a deaf man comprehend sounds, so bodies

---

[1] See Tos. Yom Tob *ad loc.*

[2] It should, however, be noted that such verses as: Num. xvi. 30; I Sam xxviii. 13–19; Is xxvi. 19 and xxxviii. 18; Job iv. 20–21, xxvi. 6 and xxx. 23; Prov. xv. 11 and xxvii. 20; Eccl. xii. 7; Dan. xii. 2; prevent us from speaking too glibly of the 'silence' of Scripture on this matter. Cf. R. H. Charles: *A Critical History of the Doctrine of a Future Life*, Lond., 1913.

[3] The details can be studied in I. Epstein's useful pamphlet, *Social Legislation in the Talmud*, Torah Va'abhodah Ideological Series (n.d.).

cannot comprehend the delights of the soul. And even as fish do not know the element fire because they exist ever in its opposite, so are the delights of the world of the spirit unknown to this world of flesh. Indeed we have no pleasure in any way except what is bodily. Anything else is non-existent for us: we do not discern it, neither do we grasp it at first thought, but only after deep contemplation. And truly this must necessarily be the case. For we live in a material world, and the only pleasure we can comprehend must be material. But the delights of the spirit are everlasting and uninterrupted, and there is no resemblance in any possible way between spiritual and bodily enjoyments. We are not sanctioned either by the *Torah* or by the divine philosophers to assert that the angels, the stars, and the spheres enjoy no delights. In truth they have exceeding great delight in respect of what they comprehend of the Creator (glorified be He!). This to them is an everlasting felicity without a break. They have no bodily pleasures, neither do they comprehend them, because they have no senses like ours enabling them to have our sense experiences. And so it will be with us too when after death the worthy from among us will reach that exalted stage'.[1] Judaism knows too of cruder conceptions but it is safe to say that no representative Jewish theologian has ever countenanced anything like the sensual 'lemonade and dark-eyed houris' sort of Heaven. We are commanded to fast on Yom Kippur, says the Zohar, to teach that the pleasures of Heaven are non-material. Many of the Rabbis, with their devotion to Torah study, believed that Heaven can best be described as the 'Academy on High', in which God himself teaches the righteous His Torah. They believed too that humans can experience a foretaste of heavenly bliss in the delights of the Sabbath of which they spoke as ' *'Olam Haba* in miniature'.

The mystics in particular have taught that *eternal* life is quite different from endless duration in Time. Eternity is outside Space and Time. Strictly speaking we err when we speak of Heaven as the *Hereafter* or the *After-life* as if it were an extension of life in Time. The world of Eternity is not in Time at all;

it is the world of Truth, the eternal *Now*, the world of Ultimate
Reality. Indeed, in this view we ought not to speak of Heaven
as a *place* but as a *state* of the soul; we ought rather to speak of
'becoming' Heaven (though even here human language pre-
vents us from escaping from the categories of Time) than of
'going' to Heaven.

> I sent my Soul through the Invisible,
> Some letter of that After-life to spell:
> And by and by my soul returned to me
> And answered 'I Myself am Heaven and Hell'.

The mystics expound too the interesting doctrine of what
they call 'bread of shame'—*nahama dekesupha*. If, they argue,
God created man so that he inherits eternal life what is the
purpose of the probationary period here on earth? Why
could God not have created man in Heaven? Their answer is
that there is a divine spark in man which refuses to be satisfied
with undeserved good; a proud individuality and independence
which causes him to reject spiritual benefits he has not earned,
in the same way that a man here on earth prefers to work for his
living than to eat 'bread of shame'. God, in other words, wants
man to share in His Goodness by freely choosing the good—we
must, indeed, go further and say that this freedom of choice is
of the essence of the good. Eternal bliss is not to be understood
so much as 'reward' for virtuous living. The pursuit of the good
here on earth is itself the creation by man of his heavenly bliss.

And, be it noted, Heaven is frequently spoken of in the Jewish
sources as a state of activity, of continuous progress in the
knowledge and the love of God. 'The best definition of Hell'
said Shaw, 'is a perpetual holiday'. The Rabbis anticipated him
when they taught that the scholars have no rest either in this
world or in the world to come.[1] Rabbi Jonathan Eibeshütz
(1690-1764) was a true disciple of theirs when he described
the ancient legend about the righteous in Heaven dancing
round God in a circle and pointing to Him and singing: 'This
is my God and I will glorify Him',[2] as a poetic way of depict-
ing the life of Heaven as an ever-increasing knowledge of

[1] Ber. 64a.
[2] Ex. xv. 2.

God. The metaphor of the circle is used, this author suggests, because the circle is finite but unbounded. The finite human mind will receive unbounded revelations of God's truth.

The strongest argument against the possibility of life beyond the grave is that the mind to all intents and purposes appears to be absolutely dependent on the brain. When the human brain is injured the human mind is affected, when the former decays the latter degenerates with it. How then, it is argued, can the mind live on after the body is no more? But the fact that the mind is dependent on the brain may only mean that it uses the brain as an *instrument*. The analogy of electricity is helpful here. Electric force can only be harnessed and used by the machinery we possess for this purpose but the force itself is quite independent of this machinery. It is not impossible that while in this life mind is dependent on the physical brain in the After-life it may not be so dependent.

H. E. Fosdick, who develops the above argument and whose statement of the religious view is altogether admirable, finely says: [1] 'If a man is riding in his limousine, he is dependent on the windows for his impression of the outside world. If the glass is covered by curtains or besmeared with mud, he cannot see. All that happens to the windows affects his power either to receive impressions from without or to signal to his friends. Yet the man is not thereby proved to be the glass, nor is it clear that he may not some day leave his limousine and see all the better because the old mediums are now discarded. A man's dependence on his instruments can never be used to prove that he is his instruments or is created by them'.

In dealing with this subject a word must be said about the Jewish doctrine of Hell. It cannot be denied that there are to be found harrowing descriptions of 'life' in Hell in the Jewish writings of the Middle Ages as well as in the writings of the Church. Although the nobler thinkers speak not of physical pain but of the tormenting deprivation of the Divine Goodness, it is difficult to reconcile God's benevolence with His condemnation of any soul to eternal torment, even of a spiritual nature. Certain it is that, on the whole, Judaism does not know of the doctrine of *eternal* punishment. And certain too that the doc-

[1] *The Assurance of Immortality*, Lond., 1936.

trine of Hell is not a dominant one in Judaism. One hears no preaching of Hell-fire in the Jewish pulpit and it is difficult to imagine a Jewish Rabbi in the last century saying, as Cardinal Newman did, that it were better for the earth and all that is in it to perish rather than that one soul should commit a single venial sin!

To sum up. As in so many other spheres Judaism steers a middle course, rejecting both extreme other-worldliness and non-attachment and hedonistic indifference to or atheistic denial of the After-life. It is, indeed, possible for a religion to be both this-worldly and other-worldly for, viewed from the aspect of Eternity, this world and the world to come are one. Eternity embraces the world of Time and what man does in the world of Time becomes his possession for all Eternity. It is this interaction between the two worlds that is at the heart of the paradox expressed by the ancient Jewish teacher: 'Better is one hour of repentance and good works in this world than the whole life of the world to come; and better is one hour of bliss in the world to come than the whole life of this world'.[1]

This chapter may fittingly conclude with a note found on the body of the American Jewish soldier Colonel David Marcus who created the Army of the State of Israel. He called it: 'The Ship' and this is what he wrote:

'I am standing upon the seashore. A ship at my side spreads her white sails to the morning breeze and starts for the blue ocean. She is an object of beauty and strength, and I stand and watch her until at length she is only a ribbon of white cloud just where the sea and sky come to mingle with each other. Then someone at my side says, "There! She's gone!" Gone where? Gone from my sight—that is all. She is just as large in mast and hull and spar as she was when she left my side, and just as able to bear her load of living freight—to the place of destination. Her diminished size is in me, not in her, and just at the moment when someone at my side says, "There! She's gone!" there are other voices ready to take up the glad shout, "There! She comes!" And that is Dying'.

---

[1] Aboth iv. 17.

CHAPTER XII

The Chosen People Idea and the Attitude of Judaism Towards Other Faiths

FEW of Judaism's teachings have been so misunderstood as the doctrine of the Chosen People. Shaw, who compared the idea to the Herrenvolk concept of the Nazis, Wells, who considered it to be a hindrance to world unity, Protestant theologians who persist in speaking of the God of Judaism as a tribal deity, as well as some Jewish groups who, with commendable universalistic zeal but doubtful historical corroboration, have removed all references to Zion from their prayer books— all attack the doctrine as retrogressive. What reply can traditional Judaism offer to these accusations? What is the traditional defence of the Chosen People idea?

Much depends on the interpretation this doctrine has received at the hands of representative Jewish teachers. It can be said without fear of contradiction that none of these teachers thought of the Jews as a nation whose destiny it is to conquer others, as a race of Supermen with the right to subdue the world. The most particularistic expressions of the Jewish spirit found in the Jewish classics are hardly ever chauvinistic. What the doctrine has meant and does mean for Jews will become clearer, it is hoped, as a result of the following considerations:

(1) The doctrine has no affinity with such notions as that of Aryan superiority. Jewish particularism is never exclusive: anyone can become a Jew by embracing the Jewish faith. Although for a long time now Judaism has not been a missionary religion it does accept proselytes. Bernard Bamberger[1] has shown conclusively that such a saying as Rabbi Helbo's: 'Proselytes are as hard for Israel as a leprous sore' is in no way typical of the Rabbinic attitude to proselytism. Some of the greatest of the Rabbis are said to have been descended from

[1] *Proselytism in the Talmudic Period,* Hebrew Union College Publications.

125

converts to Judaism. In one Talmudic passage it is said that the proselyte is dearer to God than the born Israelite. Another passage teaches that Israel was scattered among the nations only that they might make proselytes. The proselyte is regarded as a Jew in every respect. He should recite in his prayers the formula. 'Our God and the God of our fathers', for he is a spiritual child of Abraham. It is forbidden to taunt a proselyte for his former behaviour.[1]

(2) As Isaac Heinemann has proved with great erudition,[2] far from there being any contradiction between the idea of Israel's election and universalism, the former idea is inconceivable without the latter. The Biblical conception has nothing in common with the primitive notion of a tribal god protecting his own people, responding to their attempts at buying his favour and capable of suffering defeat at the hands of a more powerful deity. The relation of the tribal god to his people is a 'natural' one. He does not *choose* his people any more than they themselves are members of the tribe out of choice. In the Biblical account it is the God of all the earth who chooses Israel to His service. 'Now therefore, if ye will obey my voice indeed, and keep my convenant, then ye shall be a peculiar treasure unto me above all people: *For all the earth is mine.*'[3] 'Why sayest thou, O Jacob, and speakest, O Israel, My way is hid from the Lord, and my judgment is passed over from my God? Hast thou not known? hast thou not heard, *that the everlasting God, the Lord, the Creator of the ends of the earth,* fainteth not, neither is weary? there is no searching of his understanding'.[4] Thus saith God the Lord, *He that created the heavens, and stretched them forth, He spread forth the earth and that which cometh out of it, He that giveth bread unto the people upon it, And spirit to them that walk therein*: I the Lord have called thee in righteousness, and have taken hold of thy hand, and kept thee, and set thee for a covenant of the people, For a light of the Nations;

---

[1] For a full treatment of this subject see *Encyclopedia Talmudith*, Vol. VI, Jer. 1954, pp. 254–289.
[2] 'The Election of Israel in the Bible' (Hebrew) in *Sinai*, Vol. VIII, 1944–5 p. 17f.
[3] Ex. xix. 5.
[4] Is. xl. 27–28.

to open the blind eyes, To bring out the prisoners from the dungeon, And them that sit in darkness out of the prison-house'.[1]

(3) In the view of Israel's greatest sons, the doctrine is one that makes for service, not for privilege. In the book of Exodus Israel is described at a 'kingdom of priests'.[2] The priest was never believed to be in some mystical way superior to his fellow-Israelites. He inherited from his fathers the duty of serving his God and teaching His people. So it is with Israel. In the previous verse Israel is described as God's *segulah*.[3] This word is generally translated as 'a peculiar treasure'. Samson Raphael Hirsch, in his *Nineteen Letters*—the book in which this famous German teacher first developed the idea of the *Israel-Mensch* (the Jew serving *mankind* by living as a Jew)— notes that this designation does not imply, as some have falsely interpreted, that Israel has a monopoly of the divine love and favour, but, on the contrary, that God has the sole and exclusive claim to Israel's devotion and service; that Israel may not render Divine homage to any other being. Hirsch quotes a talmudic passage in which the word *segulah* means a property belonging exclusively to one owner, to which no other has any right or claim.[4] It might also be remarked that in this passage the word really means a 'safe investment'. Israel, as it were, is God's 'safe investment'—Israel promises to be true. Even if these interpretations are incorrect, even if they belong to homiletics rather than to sound exegesis, the fact cannot be gainsaid that the idea they express is unimpeachable. One need only think of the immortal interpretation of the Chosen People idea given by the prophet, Amos: 'You only have I known of all the families of the earth; therefore I will visit upon you all your iniquities'.[5] Or of the following typical rabbinic passage:[6] R. Johanan said in the name of R. Eleazar son of R. Simeon, Wherever you find the words of R. Eleazar the son of R. Jose the Galilean in an *Aggadah* make your ear like a funnel. It is written: "It was not because you were greater than any people that the Lord set His love upon you and chose you for you were the smallest of all peoples".[7] The

[1] Is. xlii. 5–7.   [3] Ex. xix. 5.   [5] Amos iii. 2.   [7] Deut. vii. 7.
[2] Ex. xix. 6.   [4] B.K. 87b.   [6] Hull. 89a.

Holy One, blessed is He, said to Israel, I love you because even when I bestow greatness upon you, you humble yourselves before me. I bestowed greatness upon Abraham, yet he said to Me, "I am dust and ashes";[1] upon Moses and Aaron, yet they said, "And we are nothing";[2] upon David, yet he said, "But I am a worm and no man".[3] But with the heathen it is not so. I bestowed greatness upon Nimrod, and he said, "Come let us build us a city";[4] upon Pharoah, and he said, "Who is the Lord";[5] upon Sennacherib, and he said, "Who are they among all the gods of the countries?";[6] upon Nebuchadnezzar, and he said, "I will ascend above the heights of the clouds";[7] upon Hiram king of Tyre, and he said, "I sit in the seat of God, in the heart of the seats!".".[8]

(4) The choice was reciprocal—God choosing Israel and Israel choosing God. 'Thou hast avouched the Lord this day to be thy God, and to walk in his ways, and to keep his statutes, and his commandments, and his judgments, and to hearken unto his voice: And the Lord hath avouched thee this day to be his peculiar people, as he hath promised thee, and that thou shouldest keep all his commandments'.[9]

'And Joshua said unto the people, Ye are witnesses against yourselves that ye have chosen you the Lord to serve him. And they said, we are witnesses'.[10] The Rabbis had this in mind when they spoke of God offering the Torah to all the other nations, who refused it, before giving it to Israel who accepted its yoke and cheerfully proclaimed: 'We will do and we will hear'.[11] In Zangwill's phrase: 'a chosen people is really a choosing people'.

(5) This leads to perhaps the most important consideration of all—that if the empirical test is applied it becomes obvious that no special belief in a dogma incapable of verification is here required but the recognition of sober, historical fact. The world owes to Israel the idea of the One God of righteousness and holiness. 'For only in Israel did an *ethical* monotheism

[1] Ex. xvi. 8.
[2] Gen. xviii. 27.
[3] Ps. xxii. 7.
[4] Gen. xi. 4.
[5] Ex. v. 2.
[6] II Kings xviii. 35.
[7] Is. xiv. 14.
[8] Ez. xxviii. 2.
[9] Deut. xxvi. 17–18.
[10] Josh. xxiv. 22.
[11] Sifre, Deut. xxxiii. 2.

exist; and wherever else it is found later on, it has been derived directly or indirectly from Israel, and was conditioned by the existence of the people of Israel. Hence the term the *election* of Israel expresses merely an historical fact'. (Leo Baeck.) We may agree with Maimonides that it is impossible for us to understand why God should have revealed His will to one particular nation[1] but the fact itself cannot be denied.

From what has been said it is clear that the Chosen People idea is not a narrowly exclusive one, that it is universalistic, that it invokes duty rather than bestows privileges, that it is reciprocal, and that it bears the stamp of historical truth. In sketching this outlook, frequent use has been made of quotations from the classical Jewish sources. For this no apology is required, for it cannot be too strongly emphasized that the nobler interpretations were part of the doctrine from the earliest times and are not the products of a feverish attempt by modern Jewish apologetics to disguise and render acceptable to a more critical age a tottering, decrepit doctrine, a spectre at the feast of reason. That less noble views are to be found in Jewish literature no one can deny, but Judaism, like any other faith, must be judged by its highest forms of expression. And in nearly every case the more ignoble utterances against the Gentiles were evoked by bitter religious persecutions. The Jew, incapable of retaliating by the sword, wreaked his vengeance by the pen, the voice of Jacob raised in fearful lament at the violence done by the hands of Esau.

To the question why God should have chosen one people more than another Jews have given three different answers. Many have agreed with Maimonides that all that can be said in reply to this question is that He willed it so. We cannot understand God working in this way, we would not have done it in this way if we were the creators of the world and we required our purposes to be fulfilled. But this is the whole point, that we are not God and that we cannot hope to understand the unfathomable secrets of Divine Providence.

The general rabbinic view, however, follows the thought expressed frequently in the Bible that the choice of Israel was in the merit of the Patriarchs; the doctrine of *Zekhuth 'Aboth*

[1] *Guide*, II. 25.

—the merit of the Fathers—occupying a prominent part in rabbinic theology[1] This is expressed in the prayer the devout Jew recites each morning as a prelude to his devotions:

Sovereign of all worlds! Not because of our righteous acts do we lay our supplications before thee, but because of thine abundant mercies. What are we? What is our life? What is our piety? What is our righteousness? What our helpfulness? What our strength? What our might? What shall we say before thee, O Lord our God and God of our Fathers? Are not all the mighty men as nought before thee, the men of renown as though they had not been, the wise as if without knowledge, and the men of understanding as if without discernment? For most of their works are void, and the days of their lives are vanity before thee, and the pre-eminence of man over the beast is nought: for all is vanity.

Nevertheless we are thy people, the children of thy covenant, the children of Abraham, thy friend, to whom thou didst swear on Mount Moriah; the seed of Isaac, his only son, who was bound on the altar; the congregation of Jacob, thy firstborn son, whose name thou didst call Israel and Jeshurun by reason of the love wherewith thou didst love him, and the joy wherewith thou didst rejoice in him.

It is therefore our duty to thank, praise and glorify thee, to bless, to sanctify and to offer praise and thanksgiving unto thy Name. Happy are we! how goodly is our portion, how pleasant our lot, and how beautiful our heritage! Happy are we who early and late, morning and evening, twice every day, declare: HEAR, O ISRAEL: THE LORD OUR GOD THE LORD IS ONE.

If it is true that the spirit of a religion is to be found in its liturgy then this is the dominant note in the Jewish conception of its rôle as a Chosen People—that Jews will not be false to the ideals guarded so zealously by their ancestors, that what has been preserved is of the greatest value for themselves and for mankind, and that the example of righteous forbears makes it easier for them to lead the good life.

[1] See especially S. Schechter's *Some Aspects of Rabbinic Theology*, Chapter XII, and cf. Chapter IV.

Other thinkers, again, believed that the Chosen People idea receives its validation from the unique character of the Jewish people. Judah Halevi is the most distinguished exponent of this view. For Halevi, Israel is the 'cream of the peoples', the 'heart of mankind', with a special propensity for religious experience.[1] The Kabbalists, too, speak of the special soul with which even the worst of Israelites is endowed.[2] And even such a rationalistic thinker as Abraham Geiger postulated as the basis for his philosophy of Judaism that Jews have a special genius for religion—'That conception of God', writes Geiger, 'has its sole genesis in the secret depth of the Jewish spirit and it is present as soon as that finds its expression; it is undisputed in its *entire* literature, that mouthpiece of a nation, it comes out "finished", if you so desire, from that place of its birth; like the child, even if it does grow up to manhood, it has not put itself together out of component parts thrown together from the most various points. You may call that "dropped in": I know of no genesis. God Himself is its father and Israel its mother, and you cannot find for it parents, nor even nurses wheresoever you look for them'.[3] And this view is frequently shared by admiring non-Jews. In our own day, Whitehead is reported to have said: 'The Jews as a race are probably the most able of any in existence. Now when a gifted person is charming and uses his exceptional ability generously, he is a paragon and people adore him; but in the same way, if a person with unusual ability is disagreeable, his ability makes him just so much the more disagreeable, and then the disagreeable individuals in that race are the most conspicuous'.[4] But whatever we think of such theories it is not necessary to adopt them in order to account for the election of Israel. It does appear certain that if the conventional picture of the 'brilliant young Jew' is something more than fiction, the brilliance is due to hundreds of years of Jewish struggle against adversity rather than to any innate intellectual superiority. And, as we have seen, the doctrine rests on surer grounds than these.

[1] See *Kuzari*: Part I, 27–43, 95, 101–103.
[2] *Tanya*, Chapters I and II.
[3] *Judaism and Its History*, quoted by Jacob B. Agus, *Modern Philosophies of Judaism*, p. 9.
[4] *Dialogues of A. N. Whitehead*, Lucien Price, Lond., 1954, p. 137.

Every group, if it is to preserve its distinctive values, must be convinced of the superiority of those values. The Jew who prefers the Jewish way of life above all others can as little be accused of fostering an egocentric form of particularism as those who, with good cause, wax eloquent over the British or the American way of life. In either case there is the danger of chauvinism, but which worth-while cause is not open to abuse? Rightly understood and correctly applied in the spirit of humility—and humility, national no less than individual, is among the greatest of the Jewish virtues—the Chosen People idea can be in the future the potent source of Jewish inspiration it has been in the past.

Having examined some of the more important conceptions of the Chosen People idea, we must now consider the kindred question of the attitude of Judaism towards other faiths.

There are three possible attitudes commonly held by those who, comparing one religious faith with its rivals, ask, which of them is true? Some take the view that there is only one true faith, that to which they themselves adhere, and that all the rest are false; like the old lady who said that by religion she meant the Christian religion and by the Christian religion she meant the religion of the Church of England. Others take the view that there is no difference between one religion and another. In its sceptical form this is stated to mean that all religion is false seeing that the man born in Balham is a Christian for the same reason that a man born in Calcutta is a Hindu. The third view is that of the religious believer who says there is truth in all religion but my faith possesses a greater degree of truth than any other.

The traditional Jewish attitude is the third one. While Judaism teaches that idolatry is false—the idols are spoken of in the Bible as 'elilim, literally 'things of nought', 'nonentities' —it does not assert that there is no truth in any of the doctrines or teachings of other faiths. Nor, of course, does it accept the view that the varieties of religious experience and the diverse faiths held by men is proof that religious affiliations are purely a matter of environment. It is strange that the argument that a man's faith depends on where he is born is never applied with the same implications to other aspects of human thought. No one would think of arguing that because a noted scientist or philosopher would have grown up to be a medicine man or witchdoctor had he been born in Africa instead of in London, there is no truth in science or in philosophy. We rightly claim that, while birth and environment greatly determine what a man makes of his life, there are objective tests by which the correctness of his opinions may be gauged. What reason then can there be for denying the validity of this approach in matters of religious belief? The Rabbis knew, too, that a Jewish child born in a non-Jewish environment cannot be held responsible for his failure to comply with the demands of the Jewish religion when he grows to manhood—they called such a person a 'child captured among the heathen'—and, in speaking of the saints among the nations of the world, they recognised that it is possible to live the good life outside Judaism, but they rightly saw no reason in these facts for an attitude of religious relativism.

The traditional Jewish view is that no other religion possesses so keen an insight into the truth concerning God and his relation to the world and to mankind as Judaism, and that other faiths contain erroneous ideas, but, on the other hand, even the most erudite and saintly Jew, who has progressed far in the study and practice of the Torah has, in the nature of the case, only a limited conception of the truth. This is surely implied in the frequent rabbinic panegyrics on the depth and extent of the Torah and in the idea that there are 'secrets of the Torah' to be revealed in the World to Come. The Far Eastern religions, with all the profundity of thought in some of their teachings, cannot seriously be considered as rivals of Judaism. In their cruder forms they are idolatrous, in their higher forms atheistic; quite apart from their failure to eradicate cruel and immoral practices. The attitude of Judaism to its 'daughter religions' is more complicated. Many Jewish authorities hold that these faiths are not idolatry so far as non-Jews are concerned—that is to say the good Christian or the good Muslim is a 'saint of the nations of the world'. For the Jew, however, Christianity, certainly, and Islam, possibly, are to be considered idolatrous and history informs

us how many Jews gave their lives rather than embrace these
faiths. Judaism rejects the claims made for both Jesus and
Mohammed. It teaches that the central dogma of Christianity
strikes at the roots of pure monotheism and that Islam is both
too fatalistic and has too low an ethical standard as compared
with Judaism.

But this, of course, is not to deny that Judaism considers
that there is much of value in her daughter religions. In this
connection, two passages from the writings of great Talmu-
dists have frequently been quoted and may be given here. The
first is found in uncensored manuscripts and editions of
Maimonides' great *Code of Jewish Law*.[1] Maimonides writes:
'Even of him (Jesus) who imagined that he was the Messiah
but was put to death by the Court, Daniel had previously
prophesied; as it is said, "Also the children of the violent
among thy people shall lift themselves up to establish the
vision; but they shall stumble".[2] Has there ever been a greater
stumbling than this? For all the prophets declared that the
Messiah will be the deliverer of Israel and their saviour,
gathering their dispersed ones and confirming their commandments. But he caused Israel to perish by the sword, their
remnant to be dispersed and humbled. He induced them to
change the Torah and led the greater part of the world to err
and serve another beside God. No human being, however, is
capable of fathoming the designs of the Creator, for their
ways are not His ways, neither are His thoughts their
thoughts. All these events (relating to Jesus) and even those
relating to him who succeeded the one referred to
(Mohammed), were nothing else than a means for preparing
the way for the King Messiah. It will reform the whole world
to worship God with one accord; as it said, "For then will I
turn to the peoples a pure language that they may all call upon
the name of the Lord to serve Him with one consent".[3] How
will this be? The entire world has been fitted with the doctrine of the Messiah, the Torah and the Commandments. The
doctrines have been propagated to the distant isles and among

[1] Hil. Melakhim, XI. 3–4.
[2] Dan. xi. 14.
[3] Zeph. iii. 9.

many peoples, uncircumcised of heart and flesh. They discuss these subjects which contradict the Torah. Some declare these Commandments were true, but are abrogated at the present time and have lost their force; while others assert that there are occult significations in them and they are not plain of meaning—the King has already come and revealed their hidden significance. But when the (true) King Messiah will in fact arise and succeed, be exalted and lifted up, they will immediately all recant and acknowledge the falsity of their assertions'.[1]

The second passage is found in the writings of the famous eighteenth century teacher, Jacob Emden: 'The founder of Christianity conferred a double blessing upon the world: On the one hand he strengthened the Torah of Moses, and emphasized its eternal obligatoriness. On the other hand he conferred favour upon the heathen in removing idolatry from them, imposing upon them stricter moral obligations than are contained in the Torah of Moses. There are many Christians of high qualities and excellent morals. Would that Christians would all live in conformity with their precepts! They are not enjoined, like the Israelites, to observe the Laws of Moses, nor do they sin if they associate other beings with God in worshipping a triune God. They will receive a reward from God from having propagated a belief in Him among nations that never heard His name: for He looks into the heart'.[2]

Here is the place to refer to the doctrine, developed by the Rabbis, of the 'seven commandments of the sons of Noah'; important both for the evidence it affords that the Rabbis had no exclusive dogma of 'no salvation outside the Synagogue' and for its influence on subsequent Jewish thinking concerning the relationship between Judaism and other faiths. Briefly, the doctrine is that the sons of Noah, i.e. the non-Israelites, the descendants of Noah who was saved from the deluge and became the father of the human race, are not obliged to observe all the precepts of the Torah in order to find fulfilment here on earth and merit eternal bliss in Heaven. There is

[1] Trans. by Dr. A. Cohen, quoted among others by Morris Goldstein: *Jesus in the Jewish Tradition*, N.Y., 1950, pp. 190–191.
[2] Preface to *Seder 'Olam*, 1757, quoted by Morris Goldstein, *op cit.*, p. 221.

more than one formulation of these seven precepts but that generally accepted is the following: (a) to practice justice, i.e. to formulate proper laws governing the relationship between man and his fellow, (b) not to blaspheme, (c) not to worship idols, (d) not to commit adultery or incest, (e) not to commit murder, (f) not to steal and (g) not to eat flesh cut from an animal while it is still alive. The Gentile who observes these seven precepts is termed 'a saint of the nations of the world' and he has a share in the life to come.[1]

Rabbi Joshua, whom the Synagogue follows in this matter, quoted the verse in Psalms: 'The wicked shall return to the netherworld, even all the nations that *forget God*'[2] to prove that only the nations who forget God are denied a share in the After-life, not the 'righteous of the nations'.[3] And this remained the official view of the Synagogue, expressed in an oft-quoted late Midrash: 'I bring heaven and earth to witness that the Holy Spirit dwells on a non-Jew as well as upon a Jew, upon a woman as well as upon a man, upon a maid-servant as well as upon a man-servant. All depends upon the work of that particular individual'.[4]

There is a delicate balance in Judaism between particularism and universalism, so that it is possessed of the depth of one and the breadth of the other. The Jew learned early in his history not to be afraid of non-conformity, of having a point of view of his own. He preferred to keep his ideals pure and intact even when this meant being outlawed from Gentile society. In the words of Ahad Ha'am he stayed 'in a corner' rather than pay the price of apostasy. But in his corner he did not forget the wider ideal. And in his prayers, in his dreams, in his songs and in his tears, he looked forward to the day when all mankind would call on the Name of the Lord. And to this day on the most solemn occasions in the Jewish year, on Rosh Hashanah and the great Day of Atonement when Israel meets its God, the Jew, a true disciple of the prophets prays: 'Now,

[1] See *Encyclopedia Talmudith*, Vol. III, Jer. 1951, s.v. *Ben Noah*. pp. 348–362.

[2] Ps. xi. 18.

[3] Tos. Sanh. xiii. 2.

[4] Tanna Debe Elijahu Rabba 9, Yalkut to Judges iv. 4. Cf. Bloch: *Israel and the Nations*, p. 42f.

therefore, O Lord our God, impose thine awe upon all thy works, and thy dread upon all that thou hast created, that all works may revere thee and all creatures prostrate themselves before thee, that they may all form a single band to do thy will with a perfect heart; even as we know, O Lord our God, that dominion is thine, strength is in thy hand, and might in thy right hand, and that thy Name is to be revered above all that thou hast created'.

Epilogue

THIS book created little stir when it was first published in 1957. Even those who later attacked it for containing heresy demonstrated by their silence at the time that they had either not read it at all or had found nothing in it dangerous to the Jewish faith to require refutation or denunciation.

About three years after the book's publication I began to be involved in a theological controversy, culminating first in the Chief Rabbi's veto of my appointment to the Principalship of Jews' College and later in his ban on my re-appointment to the pulpit of the New West End Synagogue. The chief ground of offence was apparently my acknowledgement of a human element in the *Torah*. Since this view had first been put forward in *We Have Reason to Believe* the book came to be looked upon as the source of the infection, deserving to be placed on the Jewish 'Index', if there were such a thing, with the inevitable result of increasing its sales and eventually producing, by popular demand, a second edition and now a third. One of the most penetrating pieces of literary criticism ever recorded is that of the little girl given a present of a book on penguins. She remarked that the book told her more about penguins than she wanted to know. The heresy hunters seemed to have held that *We Have Reason to Believe* told its readers more about the implications of Biblical Criticism than believing Jews, secure in their Orthodoxy, ought to know. An additional cause of complaint was that while the opinions expressed in the book were neither particularly novel nor startling it was perhaps the first time that they had been put down in black and white by a Rabbi belonging to what in Anglo-Jewry is described as Orthodoxy. I was frequently reprimanded for failing to heed the advice, useful in some circumstances but rather pusillanimous in others, of Rabbi Israel Salanter: 'Not

138

everything that one thinks should be spoken aloud. Not everything that is spoken aloud should be committed to writing. Not everything that is committed to writing should be published'.

The view I have tried to sketch briefly in this book and have tried to elaborate on in subsequent books, that the Jew, if he is not to stifle his reason, must be free to investigate the classical sources of Judaism with as much objectivity as he can command and should not look upon this as precluded by his religious faith, seems to me to be impregnable. Needless to say, this is not my discovery but is held by the vast majority of Jewish scholars of any academic repute. The result of such investigation, involving the use of tried methods of research, a cautious weighing of the evidence and an unbiased approach to the texts, yields a picture of the Bible and the Talmud as works produced by human beings, bearing all the marks of human literary production, influenced in style, language and ideas by the cultural background of their day. Like other human productions they contain error as well as truth. For all that, and this is the most significant part of the discussion for faith, the believer can still see the *Torah* as divine revelation. The notion of divine dictation must, of course, be abandoned, once the human element is granted, and the Bible, for example, can no longer be seen as revelation itself. But it is the *record* of revelation. The whole is a tremendous account (and for this reason unique and not simply 'inspired' in the sense in which one speaks of Shakespeare or Beethoven being inspired) of the divine-human encounter in the history of our ancestors in which they reached out gropingly for God and He responded to their faltering quest. This does not mean that we can naïvely mark (as I have been accused of trying to do) certain lofty passages as divine and others of a more primitive nature as human. In the new picture of the Bible the divine and the human are seen as intertwined. Because humans had a hand in its composition it is, from one point of view, all human. Because out of its totality God is revealed to us and speaks to us, it is, from another point of view, all divine.

My critics have repeatedly stated, without the slightest

warrant in anything I have written, that I have embraced blindly and uncritically the old-fashioned, nineteenth-century critical position, in servile deference to the dazzling guesses of arrogant, Anti-Semitic, German scholars, blissfully unaware that modern scholarship has abandoned this position. This is to miss the point entirely. No doubt much progress has been made in Biblical Criticism since the days of Wellhausen, but whether present-day scholars accept the Documentary Hypothesis (and the majority still do with various modifications) or whether they have overthrown it completely they still work by the critical method and obtain results by the application of that method at variance with the traditional view. The syllogism of some of my fundamentalist opponents appears to be:

Modern scholarship has rejected Wellhausen.
The traditional view rejects Wellhausen.
Therefore the traditional view is abreast of modern
    scholarship.

Leaving aside the dubious nature of the premise, this is akin to saying:

All men are mortal.
An elephant is mortal.
Therefore an elephant is a man.

It cannot be too strongly emphasised that the theologian, *qua* theologian, is not called upon to adopt the opinions of any one critical school. He is not obliged to take sides in the critical game but to consider the implications for his faith if the game is to be played at all. The fundamentalist theologian really holds that the game must not be played at all since the issue has been decided by tradition. Some of our fundamentalists behave like the referee who allows the players to kick the ball about according to the rules provided they score no goals.

The issue is basically a simple one. Do we prejudge every literary question in Biblical (and in Talmudic) studies by an appeal to tradition or do we sit down before the facts to ask what they teach us? To adopt the first alternative is honest, though it means that the mind is closed to all new knowledge. But to adopt it and then appeal in its support to scholars who adopt the second alternative when, and only when, their views coincide with tradition is to wish to have one's cake and eat it.

Dr. R. J. Zwi Werblowsky has put it very well ('Creative or Fundamentalist Orthodoxy?', *The Jewish Chronicle*, Feb. 9, 1962):

'The main difference between the present-day so-called Orthodox approach to the "study of things Divine" (i.e. theology, including halacha), and the spirit of modern scholarship is thus not merely a matter of specialisations. It is not a question of studying Talmud at a yeshiva and medicine at a university. The question is whether the study of the Talmud or of the Bible is held to be religiously possible only if the student shuts himself off from everything history, philology, sociology, and other sciences have to say (or, alternatively, is made to believe first that a certain brand of duly censored and bowdlerised pseudo-philology and pseudo-history is a substitute for scholarship).

'An unequivocal ruling that scholarship is *trefa* could, at a pinch, be considered a *p'sak halacha*; it would certainly be considered an honest religious choice. As such, it will be respected even by scholars. But it is clearly inadmissible to condemn the results of modern scholarship because they are heretical, i.e., on purely theological grounds, and then go on to say that anyhow they have been refuted by Orthodox scholars.

'Hearing this slightly amusing argument, which is still advanced sometimes, one does not know at what to wonder more: at the theological *naïveté* or at the scholarly incompetence which it betrays.

'Orthodox polemicists like to point out that scientific methods, insights, assumptions, and results often change. In fact, there are "fashions" in scholarship. But this is as it ought to be. Science would not be alive if it did not change, and its supreme glory is its spirit of continual self-probing and self-criticism. To oppose the changes in the history of science to the alleged permanence of religious teaching and practice is rather like opposing the permanence of a well-preserved skeleton or mummy to the changes of a living organism. Of course, religion, too, to the extent that it has been alive, has always been changing. The history of Judaism makes this truth obvious. And it is one of the tasks of the theologian to study the relationship of the abiding essence to its ever-changing manifestations'.

Some of my critics have bridled at the use of the term 'fundamentalism' to describe their position, arguing that this term, imported from Protestantism, is irrelevant to the Jewish situation. The Jewish traditionalist, it is hotly asserted, far from being committed, like the Protestant fundamentalist, to a literalist interpretation of Biblical texts, frequently understands these texts, in obedience to tradition, in a non-literal fashion. But this is a quibble. The name 'fundamentalist' was adopted by some Protestant writers in America at the beginning of this century to describe their opposition to 'liberalism'. They held, among other things, that the doctrine of the verbal inspiration of Scripture and its concomitant of Scriptural inerrancy are 'fundamentals' of faith, so that if one rejects them one might as well reject the faith as a whole. For all his emphasis on the traditional non-literal character of Scripture, the Jewish fundamentalist says exactly the same thing. Indeed, he goes further in claiming divine dictation and inerrancy for the traditions themselves. It is essential to believe, according to him, that the whole Pentateuch was dictated by God to Moses together with the traditional interpretations of its laws. The author of these is neither Moses nor any other human being but God Himself. The whole notion of development is rejected as a modern conjecture at variance with tradition and therefore to be disregarded. And unless all this is accepted, the argument runs, Judaism as a religion has neither value nor meaning. It is this either/or that those of us who are not fundamentalists find intolerable. We refuse to accept that the only choice before us is the stark one of either rejecting all modern knowledge and scholarship or rejecting belief. We believe that we can have both. It is because we have faith in Judaism that we have confidence in its power to survive without an artificial buttressing of untenable theories.

Nor has it been my aim to attempt to 'sell' Biblical Criticism. To those aware of the facts this has long been 'sold'. We ought by now to be living in the *post*-critical age, in which men, convinced of the eternal truth of their faith, are earnestly engaged in trying to understand its meaning and relevance through a theological approach which builds on sure foundations. Scholarship is itself theologically neutral. Scholarship can only provide us with the facts. It can inform us of what actually happened in the past. Our interpretation of the facts will depend in large measure on our general attitudes towards life. If we are believing Jews this will mean that we are convinced that God revealed Himself to mankind to and through the ancestors of the Jewish people and that this people still has a most significant role to play in God's world. But the facts are sacred and must not be distorted in the name of faith. The principle of faith must not be invoked in order to prejudge scholarly investigation. A theology which seeks to overlook or to reject the findings of scholarship is a bad theology and, since we believe that the seal of God is truth, one bound ultimately to fail.

Reading some of the criticisms levelled against the book one would imagine that I had called it 'We Have Belief in Reason'. I have been presented as an old-fashioned worshipper of reason who has never heard of Kant's critique and the non-rational aspects of religion, who, adapting the words of Chesterton, tries to get the heavens into his head instead of his head into the heavens. I cannot see how any reader of the book can imagine that this is the outlook I have adopted there. Certainly, faith involves a relationship of the whole person with God, not the reason alone. Certainly, it is profoundly true that God is not to be reached merely as the conclusion of an argument. The mystics, Schleiermacher, Rudolf Otto, the Existentialists and our own Rabbi Kook have not spoken in vain. But the recognition of the *non*-rational aspects of religious faith must not be confused with religious irrationalism. Faith is different from reason and transcends reason but reason is the only tool we have by which to distinguish faith from credulity, truth from superstition.

A curious reaction of another sort has been to decry theological thinking as such. Judaism is said to be a religion of action which frowns on theology as unsettling. It is difficult to take this kind of objection seriously. Systematic theological thinking came late into Judaism, but it is surely no more than escapism to avow that Judaism must never be thought about seriously, but only practised energetically. There is something oddly comforting to certain minds about an indifference to the deeper meaning of religion in the name of religion itself. But it is cold comfort that would seek to turn Judaism into a form of behaviourism. Do it and don't think too much about it is a poor programme for the heirs of Saadiah, Maimonides, Bahya and Gabirol. No one in his right senses would dream of raising intricate religious questions for the consideration of the man of simple, uncomplicated faith. But, in our day, when there is probably a larger proportion of Jews proficient in general thinking than ever before, it is folly to refuse the critical powers which have been awakened their head. Nor is it true that the inquiring spirit is bound to be hostile to Jewish observance. Naturally, there is a risk that in probing more deeply into the significance of Judaism some traditional practices may be questioned, but the risk is worth taking. The truth is that in the Western world Jewish observance is, in any event, at a low ebb. It can plausibly be argued that, together with other factors, the decline is partly the responsibility of that mechanical approach towards observance at times fostered by those suspicious of theology. A deepening in understanding and a freeing of the intellect from a restrictive fundamentalism has not infrequently resulted in a corresponding depth in appreciation of Jewish practices. Let anyone who doubts this read the biography of Franz Rosenzweig.

On this question of practice Professor Cyril Domb, for instance, has objected that once a human element is recognised in the *Torah* Jewish observance will be seriously affected and will eventually disintegrate. Writing in *The Jewish Review* (Feb. 21, 1962) Domb remarks: 'For indeed once one is prepared to concede that certain parts of the *Torah* are ephemeral, and that human beings have the right to abrogate them, the door is open to the complete disintegration of *practical* Judaism. How do we know, for example, that the command to wear a Tzitzit is eternal, or to put Mezuzot on our house, to eat only Kosher food, to live in the Succah for seven days, and all the other commandments which may cause great inconvenience and have little to do with twentieth-century society?' For those who argue in this way the only sanction for Jewish observances is that they were dictated by God to Moses. They are seen apparently as having no value, religious or otherwise, in themselves. Unless the sanction of divine dictation is safeguarded Jews will give them up because they are 'inconvenient' or 'have little to do with twentieth-century society.' But countless Jews have seen the utmost relevance to the religious life in the great religious symbols of our faith and have been and are gladly prepared to suffer the inconvenience their observance entails even if they do not believe in the doctrine of verbal inspiration. After all Jews suffer inconvenience in order to go to Synagogue even though on any showing this was not enjoined at Sinai. As for their relevance to twentieth-century society, if God is relevant to the twentieth-century or to any other society the religious practices which bring men nearer to Him are relevant. The twentieth-century has as much need of holiness as the tenth. Because of their religious value the observances, as I have argued elsewhere ('The Sanction for the *Mitzwoth*', lecture published by the Society for the Study of Jewish Theology, 1963), acquire, too, the force of a divine command, not, indeed, one conveyed by direct dictation but through the collective religious experience and history of the Jewish people.

An important issue raised in the recent controversy over this book and others like it is the question of religious authority. A number of people remarked that it was difficult for them as laymen to know which side was right. One thing, however, they argued, was clear beyond doubt. Practically all Orthodox Rabbis declared themselves to be on the side of the Chief Rabbi and the Beth Din. What was the layman to do but rely on the opinion of most of the experts against that of one or two individual Rabbis? If virtually all doctors declared in solemn pronouncement that a certain course of treatment was harmful who would dream of relying on the few doctors who declared it to be beneficial?

Now the whole business of appealing to the experts is hazardous unless we are quite sure that the men we consult are proficient in that particular field in which their advice is sought. It is one of the great heresies of modern times that eminence in one sphere of human activity gives a man the right to be heard with authority even in fields in which he has no competence. An athlete is produced to recommend a brand of toothpaste or a pop singer to advocate the virtues of religion. Certainly if nearly all Rabbis stated that a rule was to be found in the *Shulhan Arukh,* the layman would be justified, if he could not check it himself, in taking their word for it against a handful of Rabbis who claimed that the *Shulhan Arukh* said no such thing. But in the issue under discussion – the attitude one ought to adopt to the problems raised by modern methods of research into the sources of Judaism – the experts to which the layman should appeal, if appeal he must, are those who know both the sources and the method. To acquire the method, or even a close familiarity with it, one has to spend some time in a University or equivalent school of higher learning or, at the very least, to have studied thoroughly works dealing with the subject.

A recognition of this immediately reduces the number of Rabbis who are entitled to be considered experts in the field we are discussing. With very few exceptions, those Orthodox Rabbis accepted as great authorities in Jewish law today not only have scant acquaintance with critical methods but are averse to all secular studies as at best time-consuming, at worst detrimental to a wholesome *Torah* outlook. These men received their Rabbinic training in the *Beth Ha-Midrash* or in the famous Lithuanian, Polish or Hungarian *Yeshiboth.* The massive learning, the piety, the application to study, beyond anything dreamed of in the Western world, of places like Mir and Slabodka, Telz and Grodno, Pressburg and Lublin are most worthy of our admiration, but no one would pretend that the texts studied there were investigated in the spirit of objective inquiry, with the use of scientific methods, typical of a University. It is notorious, moreover, that in these great houses of learning even the 'Jewish' subjects of Bible, Jewish philosophy and Jewish history were neglected. The alumni of these institutions, the present-day Rabbis of the old school, make no secret of their contempt for secular studies for Rabbinic students and their strong and sincere conviction that salvation is only to be found in the old pattern of learning. To give one example among many, Dayan I. J. Weiss of Manchester, a foremost Halakhic authority, obviously sees little point in an institution like Jews' College for the training of Rabbis and Ministers and wishes to see established only *Yeshiboth* of the old-fashioned type from which all secular learning and scholarship have been banned. Rabbi Weiss complains in his Introduction to the latest volume of his Responsa (*Minhath Yitzhak*, Vol. III, London, 1962) that in our generation there is a neglect of *Halakhah* even on the part of Rabbis. In his opinion the blame rests squarely on those Rabbis who grant *Semikhah*, Rabbinic ordination, without first making sure that the candidate is sufficiently God-fearing to deserve the title 'Rabbi'. Rabbi Weiss continues: 'The result is that men are called "Rabbis" and "Sages" who are remote from profound *Torah* knowledge and observance of the *mitzwoth*. All their boast is in other wisdom and learning. They exchange the four ells of *Halakhah* for two thousand ells of other sciences, going beyond the limits imposed by our Sages of blessed memory. Consequently, we are obliged to repair this breach, removing this stumbling-block from beneath us, to increase *Torah* and glorify it through the true *Torah* institutions, namely, the *Yeshiboth*, the authentic *Torah* fortresses, from which alone the light that is the true *Torah* can proceed to all the communities of Israel'. I can understand, even though disagreeing with, the attitude of Rabbis like Dayan Weiss. For them the whole enterprise of combining *Torah* with *Wissenschaft* is a dangerous error. What I find hard to understand is the attitude of those laymen who support institutions like Jews' College as worthwhile for the training of Rabbis and Ministers and yet allow themselves to be influenced by Rabbis like

Dayan Weiss on what should be taught there. For Rabbis like Dayan Weiss reject the institutions themselves.

The real debate revolves around the question of how traditional Judaism is to make its impact in the Western world among those who see value in that world and do not wish to opt out of it. If the appeal to Rabbinic expertise is to be made at all in this field (and some of us would feel happier if our laymen were not quite so bent on declaring their utter incompetence) it can only be to experts who are at home both in the Western world and in the world of traditional Judaism. And here we notice a curious thing. Modern Rabbinical Seminaries such as Jews' College, Yeshiva University and the Jewish Theological Seminary are staffed by scholars of world renown and distinction. Their graduates emerge adequately equipped to cope with the kind of problem we are considering. Modern Rabbis of this sort are more or less in agreement on the value of the new methods, evolved by a host of careful and brilliant scholars over the past hundred and fifty years, for the investigation of the classical Jewish sources. It is now seen, for instance, that the Psalms, the Talmud, the Zohar, can all be studied against their background and be approached objectively and without preconceived notions, yielding results and conclusions sometimes at variance with tradition but, for all that, without detriment to the religious significance of these classics. Even the most Orthodox of modern scholars, nowadays, are prepared to accept, without adopting a pose of daring inconoclasm, that the book of Ecclesiastes, for instance, was not written by King Solomon as tradition declares. And yet the trouble starts when critical method is applied to the Pentateuch.

Many Rabbis who would have no hesitation in admitting that some of the Psalms were not, in fact, written by King David will treat as heresy the suggestion that some of the Pentateuch was not written by Moses. And the question is, of course, far more than one of authorship. It makes no difference to Jewish observance whether the Psalms were written by David or by others. Quite otherwise is it with regard to the very source of Jewish law and practice, the

Pentateuch. Once admit that tradition is mistaken in ascribing the five books of Moses to the great lawgiver, once admit that these books are not a unity but are composite, put together at different periods under different conditions, containing contradictions and subject to human error, and you open the door wide, it is claimed, to a relativistic approach to Jewish observance. Unless the absolute character of the Pentateuch as the very word of God is safeguarded there is no telling what might happen. It is for this compelling reason that many modern Rabbis, fully aware of critical theories and prepared to follow them with regard to the other Biblical books and the rest of Jewish sacred literature, feel obliged to call a halt when the *Sepher Torah*, the book revered in every Synagogue, is affected. The crime of Rabbis who think as I do is, according to their opponents, that they raise their hands irreverently against the Pentateuch, the Holy of holies, the foundation of Judaism.

Cogent though this objection may appear to be it does not bear serious investigation. If the *method* is sound its progress cannot be arrested. The overwhelming majority of modern scholars arrive at the new picture of how the Pentateuch came to be by the very same methods they use to determine how the book of Ecclesiastes came to be. If tradition is an adequate and infallible guide in the one case it must be so in the other. Any half-way house is an artificial resting place offering neither hospitality nor security for the weary traveller. The logic is with Dayan Weiss. On the analogy of medicine it is as if many doctors persisted in applying modern methods of cure for complaints of the nose, ear and throat but lacked confidence in modern medicine when it came to diseases of the brain and heart. The layman will hardly accept the opinions of those healers who treat the whole of modern medicine as a mistake. By the same token he will have no confidence in those doctors who betray their own lack of confidence by imposing arbitrary limits on their craft.

Many worthy people are, however, puzzled by the view that parts of the Pentateuch are post-Mosaic and that many of its laws were formulated in response to conditions which arose long after (or in some cases long before) Moses' day. What then is to be made of the words by which many of the Pentateuchal laws are prefaced: 'And the Lord spake unto Moses'? Does this not mean that those who used these words to introduce later laws were acting in bad faith, perpetrating a pious fraud by invoking the name of the ancient lawgiver? Before we consider the reply to this question it should be noted that the fundamentalist is also faced with a severe problem in these words. For if he upholds, as he must, the traditional view then the words: 'And the Lord spake unto Moses' were *themselves* spoken to Moses, a claim which, it hardly needs pointing out, the Pentateuch does not itself make. For on the fundamentalist view every word and every letter of the Pentateuch had God as its Author and the words: 'And the Lord spake unto Moses' are included.

In reality the objection which calls into question the good faith of the later writers is due to a misunderstanding of the thought patterns of the ancient Hebrews as well as of how all law develops. There are a number of good accounts of why later laws were ascribed to Moses, a device used, incidentally, by the Rabbis when they say that whatever a keen student of the *Torah* is destined to discover in his *Torah* investigations was given to Moses on Sinai. One of the best of these accounts is that of Professor H. Wheeler Robinson in his book: *Inspiration and Revelation in the Old Testament* (Clarendon Press, Oxford, Paperback ed., 1962). Wheeler Robinson notes that the ancient Hebrews were much more interested in result than in process. What mattered to them was not how a law or an idea or a psalm came to be but that it had come to be and was now part of their life's pattern under God. The great figures of the past acted as magnets for later developments of the ideas they had originated. Thus, all Wisdom was ascribed to Solomon, all Psalmody to David, and, in exactly the same way, all Law to Moses. The law as applied to new conditions could be said to be *given* as part of the old law even when this meant that new laws had been formulated. There is nothing peculiar about this to students of legal history. English common law, for example, has developed in exactly the same way. It is conceivable that in prophecy, too, all later messages might have been ascribed to some great prophet of the past such as Elijah. That this did not happen can be explained as due to the far more personal nature of prophecy. The personality of the prophet, his individuality, is far more involved in both his vision and his message than the personality of the lawmaker in his laws. Law by its very nature is impersonal. But just as the prophet is moved by his experience to declare that the Lord had delivered the message to him so is the lawmaker moved to declare that the Lord had delivered the law to Moses. The important thing for both lawmaker and prophet was that they discerned the hand of God in human affairs, the one on the elevated plane of prophetic vision, the other on the less elevated, but no less significant, plane of ordinary day-to-day living. The words: 'And the Lord spake unto Moses' are thus seen as the counterpart of the prophetic: 'Thus saith the Lord'. The one is as much a sincere prefatory formula as the other. The picture of crafty priests consciously pretending that laws of their own invention had divine sanction in order to foist them on a credulous people is sheer fabrication and devoid of any historical substance.

Finally, those critics who described the book as 'popular' were right. It was never intended to be anything else. It was presented as a very small contribution towards a discussion of much significance. I do not myself look upon the 'popular' as beneath the concern of the serious. It is in many ways harder to write a popular book with clarity than a learned one. But by all means let there be more learned discussions of the weighty themes *We Have Reason to Believe* considers on the popular level. Only by thinking about our Judaism as seriously and as rigorously as we do about less important (from the point of view of ultimate concern) matters can we hope to present our religion as the challenging, relevant, sublime faith it is.

Bibliography

The following list of books and articles for further reading makes no attempt to provide anything like a complete and comprehensive bibliography on the subjects treated in this book. All the works listed are in English with the exception of a few in Hebrew to which reference has been made in the text.

ABELSON, J.: 'Maimonides on the Jewish Creed.' *Jewish Quarterly Review*, Old Series, Vol. XIX, 1907, pp. 24f.
The Immanence of God in Rabbinical Literature, Lond., 1912.
ABRAHAM, Karl: 'The Day of Atonement.' Some observations on Reik's 'Problems of the Psychology of Religion,' in *Clinical Papers and Essays on Psycho-Analysis*, Lond., 1955, p. 137f.
AGUS, Jacob B.: *Modern Philosophies of Judaism*. A study of recent Jewish philosophies of Religion. New York, 1941.
Guideposts in Modern Judaism. New York, 1954.
ALBO, Joseph: *Sefer Ha-'Ikkarim*, trans. by Isaac Husik, Phil., 1929.
ALTMANN, A.: *Saadya Gaon*. The Book of Doctrines and Beliefs. Oxford, 1946.

BAECK, Leo: *The Essence of Judaism*. Lond., 1936.
BAMBERGER, Bernard J.: 'Revelations of Torah after Sinai,' in *Hebrew Union College Annual*. Vol. XVI, 1941, p. 97f.
BARON, Salo W.: *A social and religious history of the Jews*, 2nd ed. New York, 1952.
BARTH, A.: *Dorenu Mul She'eloth Ha-Netzah*, 2nd ed. Jer., 1955.
BETTAN, Israel: *Studies in Jewish Preaching*. Cincinnati, 1939.
BEVAN, Edwyn R. and Singer, Charles: *The Legacy of Israel*. O.U.P., 1928.
BLAMIRES, H.: *The Faith and Modern Error*. Lond., 1956.
BLOCH, Joseph S.: *Israel and the Nations*. Berlin, 1927.
BROAD, C. S.: *Religion, Philosophy and Psychical Research*. Selected essays. Lond., 1953.
BROWNE, Lewis: *This Believing World*. New York, 1927.
BUBER, Martin: *Eclipse of God*. Studies in the relation between religion and philosophy. Lond., 1953.

CASSUTTO, M. D.: *The Documentary Hypothesis* (Heb.), 2nd ed. Jer., 1953.

CHARLES, R. H.: *A Critical History of the Doctrine of a Future Life.* Lond., 1913.

COHEN, Abraham: *The Teachings of Maimonides.* Lond., 1927. *Everyman's Talmud.* Lond., 1932. *The Parting of the Ways. Judaism and the Rise of Christianity.* Lond., 1954.

COPLESTON, Frederick, S. J.: *Contemporary Philosophy.* Lond., 1956.

CRAIG, A. C.: *Preaching in a Scientific Age.* Lond., 1954.

CRONBACH, Abraham: 'Psychoanalytic Study of Judaism,' in *Hebrew Union College Annual,* Vol. VIII-IX, 1931-2.

DAUBE, David: *The New Testament and Rabbinic Judaism.* Lond., 1956.

DESSLER, A. A.: *Mikhtab Me-Elijahu.* Lond., 1955.

DRIVER, S. R.: *Notes on the Hebrew Text of the Books of Samuel.* Oxford, 1890.

DRUYANOV, Alter: *Studies, in Reshumoth,* Vol. I, Odessa, 1918, pp. 199–204; Vol. II, Tel Aviv, pp. 303–357.

ELLIOT-BINNS, L. E.: *Religion in the Victorian Era,* Lond., 1946.

EPSTEIN, I.: *Judaism.* Lond., 1939. *The Faith of Judaism.* An Interpretation for our Times. Lond., 1954.

EWING, A. C.: *The Fundamental Questions of Philosophy.* Lond., 1951.

FARBRIDGE, Maurice H.: *Judaism and the Modern Mind.* New York, 1927.

FINKELSTEIN, Louis: ed. *The Jews, Their History, Culture and Religion.* Vol. I and II. Phil., 1949.

FREUD, S.: *Totem and Taboo.* 1913. *The Future of an Illusion.* 1928. *Moses and Monotheism.* 1939.

FRIEDLÄNDER, M.: *The Jewish Religion.* Lond., 1953.

FRIEDMAN, Maurice S.: *Martin Buber, The Life of Dialogue.* Lond., 1955.

FOSDICK, H. E.: *The Assurance of Immortality.* Lond., 1936.

GINZBERG, Louis: *Students, Scholars and Saints.* Phil., 1928. *The Legends of the Jews.* Phil., 1942.

GLATZER, Nahum H.: *Franz Rosenzweig, His Life and Thought*. New York, 1953.
GOLDMAN, Solomon: *The Book of Books, An Introduction*. Phil., 1948.
In the Beginning. N.Y., 1949.
The Ten Commandments, edited by Maurice Samuel. University of Chicago Press, 1956.
GOLDSTEIN, Morris: *Jesus in the Jewish Tradition*. New York, 1950.

HALEVI, Judah: *Kitab Al Khazari*, trans. from the Arabic by Hartwig Hirschfeld. Lond., 1931.
HEINEMANN, Isaac: *Ta'ame Ha-Mitzvoth*. Jer., 1949.
'The Election of Israel in the Bible' (Heb.), *Sinai*, 1944–5, p. 17f.
HELLER, Bernard: 'About the Judeo-Christian Tradition', *Judaism*, Vol. I, 1952, p. 257f.
'The Judeo-Christian Tradition Concept: Aid or Deterrent to Goodwill?', *Judaism*, Vol. II, 1953, p. 133f.
HERBERG, Will: *Judaism and Modern Man*. New York, 1952.
HERTZ, J. H.: *Commentary to the Pentateuch*. Lond., 1938.
Commentary to the Prayer Book. Lond., 1947.
HESCHEL, A. J.: *Man Is Not Alone*. New York, 1951.
HIRSCH, S. R.: *The Nineteen Letters of Ben Uziel*. Trans. by Bernard Drachman, New York 1899.
HIRSCHENSON, Hayyim: *Malki Ba-Kodesh*. St. Louis, 1919-1921.
HUSIK Isaac: *A History of Mediaeval Jewish Philosophy*. Phil., 1941.

JAMES, William: *The Varieties of Religious Experience*. Lond., 1902.
JOAD, C. S.: *The Recovery of Belief*. Lond., 1952.
JOSEPH, Morris: *Judaism as Creed and Life*. Lond., 1903.
JUNG, C. G.: *Modern Man in Search of a Soul*. Lond., 1947.

KAPLAN, Mordecai M.: *Judaism as a Civilisation*. New York, 1935.
The Meaning of God in Modern Jewish Religion. New York, 1937.
KOHLER, K.: *Jewish Theology—Systematically and Historically Examined*. New York, 1928.

LEHRMAN, S. M.: *The Jewish Design For Living*. Lond., 1951.
LEVINE, Ephraim: ed. *The Jewish Heritage*. Lond., 1955.

LEVINTHAL, Israel H.: *Judaism, An Analysis and an Interpretation*. New York, 1935.
LEWIS, C. S.: *The Problem of Pain*. Lond., 1940.
Miracles. 'A Preliminary Study.' Lond., 1947.
The Screwtape Letters. Lond., 1950.
LUZZATTO, Moses Hayyim: *Mesillat Yesharim*, The Path of the Upright,' Crit. Ed., ed. by Mordecai M. Kaplan, Phil., 1936.

MACKIE, J. L.: 'Evil and Omnipotence,' *Mind*, Vol. LXIV, April, 1955, p. 200f.
MAIMONIDES, Moses: *The Guide For The Perplexed*, trans. from the original Arabic Text, by M. Friedländer, 1904.
MALTER, Henry: *Saadia Gaon His Life and Works*. Phil., 1942.
MARGOLIS, Max L.: *The Hebrew Scriptures in the Making*. Phil., 1922.
The Story of the Bible Translations. Phil., 1917.
MARMORSTEIN, A.: *The Old Rabbinic Doctrine of God*. O.U.P., 1927.
Studies in Jewish Theology, ed. by J. Rabbinowitz and M. S. Lew, O.U.P., 1950.
MAYBAUM, Ignaz: *The Jewish Mission*. Lond., 1938.
MONTEFIORE, C. G. and Loewe, H.: *A Rabbinic Anthology*. Lond., 1938.
MORGENSTERN, Julian: *As A Mighty Stream*, 'The Progress of Judaism Through History'. Phil., 1949.
MOORE, G. F.: *Judaism in the First Centuries of the Christian Era*. C.U.P., 1930.

PARKES, James: *Judaism and Christianity*. Lond., 1948.
The Foundations of Judaism and Christianity, London, Vallentine, Mitchell, 1960.
PATON, H. J.: *The Modern Predicament*. Lond., 1955.
PFEIFFER, Robert H.: *Introduction to the Old Testament*. Lond., 1953.
PHILP, H. L.: *Freud and Religious Belief*. Lond., 1956.

REIK, Theodor: *Ritual*. Lond., 1931.
Dogma and Compulsion, 'Psychoanalytic Studies of Religion and Myths.' New York, 1951.
ROBERTSON SMITH, W.: *The Old Testament in the Jewish Church*. Edinburgh, 1881.

Ross, J.: *The Jewish Conception of Immortality and the Life Hereafter*, 'An Anthology.' Belfast, 1948.
Roth, Leon: *The Guide For The Perplexed*. Lond., 1948.
God and Man in the Old Testament. Lond., 1955.
Rowley, H. H.: ed. *The Old Testament and Modern Study*, 'A Generation of Discovery and Research.' O.U.P., 1951.

Schaer, Hans: *Religion and the Cure of Souls in Jung's Psychology*, Trans. by R. F. C. Hall. Lond., 1951.
Schechter, Solomon: *Some Aspects of Rabbinic Theology*. Lond., 1909.
Studies in Judaism. Phil., 1945.
Scholem, Gershom G.: *Major Trends in Jewish Mysticism*, 3rd ed. Lond., 1955.
Schwartz, Martin H.: *Foundations of Jewish Belief*. New York, 1947.
Sevin, S.: *'Ishim We-Shittoth*. Jer., 1952.
Simon, M.: *Jewish Religious Conflicts*. Lond., 1950.
Steinberg, Milton: *The Making of the Modern Jew*. Indianapolis, 1933.
A Believing Jew. New York, 1951.
Basic Judaism. New York, 1947.
Anatomy of Faith, ed. with an Introduction by Arthur A. Cohen, New York, 1960.

Thouless, Robert H.: *Authority and Freedom*. Lond., 1954.
Tillich, Paul: 'Is There a Judeo-Christian Tradition?' *Judaism*, Vol. I, 1952, p. 160f.
Trueblood, David Elton: *Philosophy of Religion*, Lond., 1957.

Van der Leeuw, G.: *Religion In Essence and Manifestation*, trans. by J. E. Turner. Lond., 1938.

Waxman, Myer: *A History of Jewish Literature*, 2nd ed. New York, 1938–1947.
Weatherhead, Leslie D.: *Psychology, Religion and Healing*. Lond., 1952.
Weiss-Rosmarin, Trude: *Judaism and Christianity: The Differences*. New York, 1943.
Wellisch, E.: *Isaac and Oedipus*. Lond., 1954.
White, Victor: *God and the Unconscious*. Lond., 1953.

YELLIN, D. and ABRAHAMS, I.: *Maimonides*. Phil., 1946.

ZANGWILL, Israel: *Chosen People*: 'The Hebraic Ideal *Versus* the Teutonic.' New York, 1919.

ZEITLIN, Solomon: *Maimonides*, 'A Biography.' 2nd ed. New York, 1955.

ZIMMELS, H. J.: *Magicians, Theologians and Doctors*. Lond. 1952.

Seeker of Unity
Louis Jacobs

This book deals with the life and thought of an original but neglected religious thinker who, perhaps more than any other in the history of Jewish thought, grappled with the problems inherent in the idea of God's unity.

Rabbi Aaron Horowitz is generally acknowledged to be the most outstanding, systematic exponent of the profound *Habad* theory of Hasidism. With the renewed interest in Jewish mysticism and Hasidism, this work can serve as an excellent introduction to the more intricate and stimulating ideas of the Movement. Dr Jacobs has succeeded in bringing a vanished world to life for the modern reader.

2006   176 pages
0 85303 591 1   paper   £15.95/$24.95

Studies in Talmudic Logic
Louis Jacobs

Traditionally, the subjects of Talmudic logic and methodology are treated together. With a few notable exceptions, there has been little systematic presentation of the structure of the Talmudic arguments, the division of the *sugya* into its component parts, the methods of Talmudic reasoning, and the literary style and character of the Amoraic debates.

The book sheds light on Talmudic logic, in particular suggesting the ancients were aware of Induction. It then examines the analysis of the Amoraic literature, arguing that the *Gemara* in its present form is a 'contrived' literary product of great skill.

Although the book is aimed at students of the Talmud it may be of interest to the layman who desires a closer acquaintance with the full flavour of Talmudic reasoning.

'Immensely knowledgeable and elegantly argued, a groundbreaking exploration of logical structures and literary device in the Talmud: essential reading for the serious student.'

Rabbi Jonathan Wittenberg
New North London Masorti synagogue

2006   176 pages
0 85303 587 3   paper   £17.95/$27.95

Tract on Ecstasy
Louis Jacobs

Dobh Bear of Lubavitch (1773–1827), the author of *Tract on Ecstasy*, assumed the leadership of the Hasidic sect of *Habad* on the death of his father, Schneor Zalman of Liady. The *Tract* is in the form of a letter, sent by Dobh Baer to his followers, advising them on the role of ecstasy in the religious life. His thesis is that those who decry ecstasy are wrong, and that there is no such thing as a de-personalised state of contemplation in which the self does not feel anything. Dobh Baer refutes the charge that because ecstasy involves self-awareness it is therefore a betrayal of *Habad* teaching, and in the *Tract* provides a penetrating analysis of true ecstasy.

The *Tract* was originally written c.1814, and this book is based on a manuscript copy, probably written by Dobh Baer's chief scribe. The reader will hear through these pages the voice of one who was an adept, to use his own terminology, in listening to 'the words of the living God'.

2006   208 pages
0 85303 590 3   paper   £14.95/$22.95

Jewish Preaching
Homilies and Sermons
Louis Jacobs

Rabbi Jacobs, with sixty years' experience of pulpit work to his credit, provides a number of homilies for each weekly portion of the modern sermon and for the chapters of *Ethics of the Fathers*. The text for the modern sermon is usually the Sidra, the weekly portion, or in the summer months the Talmudic book known universally as *Ethics of the Fathers*. Among the sermonic themes are contemporary problems, the religious and ethical needs of the individual, and, of course, the impact of the Holocaust and the State of Israel.

248 pages
0 85303 561 X cloth £37.50/$59.50
0 85303 565 2 paper £16.95/$26.95